The Lifestyle Business Rockstar!

The Lifestyle Business Rockstar!

Quit your 9-5, kick ass, work less, and live more!

Rasmus Lindgren

Infospray Media

Dedication

To Oliver, Cecilie, and Natascha—
the loves of my life

Contents

INTRO

"As a rockstar, I have two instincts: I want to have fun, and I want to change the world. I have a chance to do both."

~ Bono

There's something about the rockstar mentality that fascinates people—it doesn't make any difference if you're young or old, rich or poor, black or white.

The rockstar lifestyle is a universal desire.

Wherever I go or whomever I meet or coach on the topic of Lifestyle Business Design, the topic of living like a rockstar often enters into the discussion.

So, who wants to be a rockstar? Apparently, everyone! Rockstar wannabes may be CEOs of Fortune 500 companies, or entrepreneurs in the world of janitorial cleaning supplies. They may be trust-fund babies looking to invest, or schoolteachers hoping to retire early. No matter what language they speak, they end up saying the same thing—*I want to live like a rockstar.*

When I ask them what that means, their responses are similar:

- *I want to be my own boss.*
- *I want to do what I love every day.*
- *I want to spend more time with my family.*
- *I want to travel.*
- *I want to wake up in a new town each morning.*
- *I want MY life to take center stage.*
- *I want to have the freedom to go where I want to go.*

Boil it down, and it comes down to this—when people say they want to live the rockstar life, it's not about the sex, drugs, or rock 'n roll. It's not about the big hair, guitar picks, or spending all of your time with roadies and sound technicians.

It's about life unplugged.

It's about a life away from cubicles, desks, and fax machines. It's about life away from deadlines, due dates, and deliverables. It's about not looking at the same mailbox every morning, and the same television each night.

It's about freedom. As I travel the world living my own rockstar lifestyle, I discover freedom is in very small supply for most people. Maybe it is for you, too—you can change that, though.

Are you ready to take your own freedom ride?

———————

The backstory . . .

My name is Rasmus Lindgren.

I was a rockstar. Well, sort of—I play piano and drums. Does that count?

I'm thirty-six, and I live in Denmark with my family—but there was a time in my not-so-distant past when I produced music. During those years, I somehow managed to receive several gold and platinum records for the work I did with several of my groups. So while I never killed a ten-minute guitar solo in front of a stadium of adoring fans, I do know a little—okay, a lot—about the rockstar lifestyle.

While on a break with my girlfriend in Thailand a few years back, I tucked a little light reading in my bag—*The 4-Hour Workweek* by Timothy Ferriss.[1]

No—really. Reading it made me think—*what can I do differently to have more freedom in my life?* I knew I loved Thailand, and I wanted to do more than just vacation there for a few weeks every year. Denmark's winters are brutal, and the thought of a warm climate fueled my desire to be in charge of my own life.

My freedom.

How can I find a job that will allow me to split my time between Denmark and Thailand each year? What kind of work can I do to allow freedom, and not chain me to a desk?

Well, those questions inspired me to change my life. I began to think differently about the way I did things—how I worked, how much I worked, and how I could work less. And live more. Although I was no longer a rockstar type, I still wanted to live like one, and I wanted more freedom in my life. I craved the ability to choose where to live, for how long, and in what style. I needed to have more time with my girlfriend and our growing family—I yearned for walks in the woods or on the beach.

But I always had to work.

I'd had it! I decided my holiday in Thailand would be my last—next time I returned from Denmark, it would be to find a semi-permanent residence, and to stay for more than just a few

[1] Crown Archetype, 2007

weeks. One drawback, though. To do that, I needed to rethink how I lived my life. Remember those questions I asked myself about how hard I worked, how smart I worked, and how I needed to find a way to put my rockstar lifestyle to work? Yep, those questions needed some answers . . .

I knew I wanted technology in the mix, because it was one of my skills that could quickly be remote for my clients and me. But what kind of technology, and how could I provide it in a way that was unique and personal?

I began freelancing as an IT consultant, and I immediately began working fewer months each year because my career as a consultant snagged higher paychecks. Most of my work was online—finding and serving clients. Skype, email, and other technology tools allowed me to work from across the street or from across the world. And, the freedom to work from home (or, anywhere!) allowed me to focus on the next step of my new, rockstar lifestyle plan.

My success as an IT consultant was the catalyst for my creating a company that delivered ecommerce solutions to small and mid-sized companies in Denmark. Later, I opened another business targeting the Danish market that offered search engine optimization (SEO) on a subscription basis.

As I evolved from consultant to business owner, my businesses began to flourish. I blogged about my experiences online and, unexpectedly, it led to my first coaching clients. They contacted me via the blog, asked questions, and eventually asked me for formal, professional advice on a fee basis. It was an evolution I didn't expect, but I quickly realized and seized an opportunity to share my expertise as a business owner and IT consultant while inspiring others to create their own lifestyle businesses.

Finally, I could take my act on the road, live wherever I wanted, and support my family with my lifestyle businesses. Did I make a few mistakes along the way? Sure. Was I surprised by parts of the rockstar lifestyle? Sure. Was there was a learning curve? Sure. Did it stop me?

Nope.

I'm passionate about teaching and coaching other people, helping them grow. Because I live the rockstar lifestyle, my passion is sharing my knowledge about how you can achieve your professional and personal rockstar lifestyle.

You're probably wondering what makes me so different than other consultants and coaches. I know I would be. Well, here's the deal—consultants and coaches can inspire. My difference? I work hard to inspire and *inform* my clients, as well.

My family includes my loving girlfriend, Natascha, our wonderful little princess, Cecilie, and our baby boy, Oliver. In the summer of 2010, we realized our lifelong dream by purchasing a second home in Thailand. My plan works for me, and I know it will work for you!

I achieved my goals—I could live anywhere or do anything with the people I love, freely and without stress. Every minute. Every day. Every year.

I learned to automate parts of my life, focus on others, and to rise to the occasion for a conference call when necessary. I learned to enjoy creative bursts three or four times a day. And, while this is what I do, I don't *have* to do it anymore. My businesses are earning money passively, whether I tend to them daily or not. So, when I do sit in front of the computer, it's typically because I'm working on a new, fun venture—such as this book!

It's then I truly feel like a rockstar . . .

HOW TO LIVE THE ROCKSTAR LIFESTYLE

Warning: this book will not teach you how to be a rockstar!

I love to play the piano and bang on the drums, but I don't know how to play the guitar—well, other than air guitar. However, I do know one thing that's crucial to living the rockstar lifestyle—*how to squeeze the most out of a lifestyle I love, live like a rockstar, and tour all year long.* Notice I haven't said anything about becoming a millionaire, buying a yacht, or retiring completely. This isn't one of those books. Since you're reading *The Lifestyle Business Rockstar*, chances are you're not one of those readers, either.

I have a feeling you're here because you're tired—tired of the grind, bills, and deadlines. You're tired of the commute, pressure, and stress. I have a feeling you're ready for change, but perhaps you're unsure of how to change, what to change, and how much to change. The good news is you're not alone. That's how I felt in 2008 when I started my first lifestyle business, and I hope this book will be as inspiring for you as writing it was for me.

Not long ago, I was sitting right where you are.

So I made a conscious decision to change. No, I'm not a millionaire, and I may never be a millionaire. But I'm living my own personal rockstar lifestyle, and my life comes first. More than money. And, for me, that's the best lifestyle money can buy.

Maybe it's because I'm growing older, or because I have a family of my own. Maybe my realizing I won't become a 'real' rockstar made me understand what I wanted out of life wasn't fame and fortune, but another equally important 'F' word—*freedom*.

That's what this book is about—the freedom to allow your lifestyle to take precedence over your workstyle, as well as the ability to do what you love—to live the lifestyle you crave. It's about relearning the American dream and discovering no one ever got rich, or free, from working nine to five.

This book provides the knowledge you'll need to live the lifestyle you want—not just in theory, but in practice, as well. By implementing several simple tools including the Rockstar Trifecta and a section about Designing Your Lifestyle Business, you'll learn how to create a work-anywhere profession in which you can earn more income by performing less work.

You don't need to invest your life savings, go back to school, or sell the house. You can be a part-time rockstar or a fulltime rockgod touring all year, if that's your rockstar lifestyle dream. Understand, however, it won't happen overnight—but, if you make the commitment to change your life now, a year from now, you'll understand how different and big your world can be.

I know, because it's happened to me. And now I'd like nothing more than to help make it happen for you.

PART 1

The Lifestyle Lie

Chapter One

What if Everything You Know about Work Is a Lie?

"Choose a job you love, and you will never have to work a day in your life."

~Confucius

Remember how you felt when you found out Santa Claus isn't real? The Tooth Fairy? The Easter Bunny? I do—it was a punch in the gut, a betrayal of all I hoped for, believed, and trusted. I was mad at the world, my parents, and the friends who gleefully clued me in and delighted in the shocked, saddened, and colorless look on my face.

That's how I feel every night when I watch the news. Every time politicians are involved in scandals, I feel as if they're lying to me. Every time I hear one pundit tell me the economy is in recovery—and the next one informs me we're headed for a third or fourth recession (I can't keep track anymore), I feel as if they're lying. Every time I watch a documentary or 'special report' on the housing, credit, or the Bernie Madoff scandal, I feel as if they're all lies.

I feel betrayed.

And I have a feeling I'm not alone.

THE GREAT LIFESTYLE LIE!

One of the comforts of growing up in the free world is the knowledge if you work hard enough and do the right thing, you will reap your rewards. If you punch the clock, endure the grind, or shovel enough paperwork from the inbox to the outbox, you will reap your rewards. The same goes if you put up with your stupid boss—life will reward you. It will reward you with what you consider your birthright—the life you've always wanted.

You'll retire with that gold watch, your house will be yours, and your pension secure. The stocks you invested in will be solvent, your IRA and 401(k) will be bursting, and you'll finally be able to live the lifestyle you always imagined—carefree days, relaxing nights, and time to spend with family and friends. You'll travel and live the good life.

The recession and its aftermath, the double dip, and the endless slog through our life's savings— stocks, 401(k)s, IRAs—and the generally prolonged dry spell blanketing the planet for the last few years perpetuate what I call 'the great lifestyle lie'.

Our teachers and parents sold us a bill of goods because they grew up with the same lie. Our government, who is at the mercy of the powerful corporate lobbyists, lies to us. Unfortunately, the status quo worked and the lie sounded good— everything appeared to be in balance. But as the recent economic downturn(s) clearly shows, balance is a precarious thing and when the world goes out of whack, it can take years—decades—to balance again. Which is fine for the fat cats and one percent who make the rules and sell the great lifestyle lie. But what about the rest of us? What are we supposed to do until the economy recovers? Now that our savings are wiped out, stocks depleted, and our 401(k)'s bankrupt, do we start over at thirty? Forty? Fifty?

The great lifestyle lie is this—you can be safe, secure, and happy while working on the corporate plantation. You'll reap the benefits by putting in your hours and years. What you don't make on your own, you can augment with your earnings from Social Security, a work pension, stock portfolio, IRA, or 401(k).

That's the lie—the *fact* is you can *never* become rich if you're mired in a nine-to-five job. Period! Why? Because you're leveraging your time and selling it for money—and this can never scale. I don't like the idea of having to struggle my entire life, retire with two false hips, and only then have time to live the life I crave.

Do you?

And yet we've lived this lie for so long, we're uncertain about the future. We're uncertain about making the switch from believing the lifestyle lie to facing the truth—and living with the knowledge safety and security are dreams of the past. Fact is, they vanish when you're working nine to five for someone else.

Here's the deal—we're happy as long we're safe even if that means working our entire lives. The problem is during the recent recession we realized employment is not for life—and, we're not safe in our jobs anymore. Tenure is certainly a crapshoot, and the promise of a relaxing retirement ranks with the Santa Claus, Tooth Fairy, and Easter Bunny thing.

Not good.

WE'RE IN THE SAME BOAT!

Unlike other recessions or depressions, this stagnant economy cuts a wide swath across myriad demographics—and it's not just individuals, families, or geographic areas—entire countries are falling prey to the economic downturn, and European economic troubles dominate the news each year.

The news is sobering and personal—many parents lose their life's savings in the stock market, and they often need to find work to help support rising medical, insurance, and housing costs. Like me, you probably watched friends, family, or coworkers, suffer through months and years of decline in their personal and professional fortunes. Laid off. Hours cut. Reassigned. Maybe their houses plummeted in value, or they missed a few payments. Maybe they had to get involved in a 'short sale' or lost their homes to foreclosure. Maybe they gave up and moved on.

The trickle-down effect reverberates through nearly every household I know. Spouses who used to coexist happily in a one-income family have now gone back to work. Former retirees compete with newly-minted MBA grads in the professional job market, or with summer-job teens in the retail and food industries. And, while seniors are feeling more than anxious about their own uncertain futures, the middle aged and the middle class view their futures in a far different context than five short years ago.

And what of our children? Will they know more about the fragile state of the world economy than the previous generation? How will they feel about the future, and how can we avoid lying to them about it? One thing is certain—our children may not care about it now, but, sooner or later, they're going to care. Now that I have children, I know it's my job to make certain they know the state of the economy. It's my job to teach them what they have to know in order to make successful lives for themselves—and, how to achieve earning passive income so they can enjoy their lives. Who knows what they'll chose to do in life, but whatever it is, they'll know how to leverage their time, money, and mobility.

BIRTH OF THE LIFESTYLE
BUSINESS ROCKSTAR!

Who will fortune favor in this new economy? Here's a clue—it's not for the squeamish. You and I know regardless of when this much-touted recovery begins, things won't be the same. Think about it— will your house be worth what you paid? Will you trust the stock market again? Will you go back to a single-family income household?

If you can't answer these questions with a resounding yes, then I think we're on the same page. The fact is what's wounded us the most—beyond our bruised financial portfolios, declining finances, and depleted savings accounts—is a shattering security.

You don't need to have a pink slip handed to you to recognize all of our necks are on the chopping blocks every day. That's if you continue to work in the corporate world.

Imagine putting the last ten, twenty, or thirty years into a company—working steadily up the ladder and banking on the company's retirement plan. Then imagine your company goes bankrupt, reorganizes, or downsizes. It goes in another direction and lets you go.

The carpet yanks out from under you.

But, it doesn't have to be that way! We can adapt, overcome, and evolve. We see the future—a future that warns us to wake up and be alert. A future that encourages us to think differently.

And that's what we'll be doing in this book . . .

Chapter Two
That was Then, This is Now
The New (Online) Business Owner

*"If what you are doing is not moving you
toward your goals, then it's moving you away from
your goals."*
~ Brian Tracy

I f not nine to five, then what? Well, if you haven't
guessed it by now, this book is going to be about
starting your own business. But before you break
into a cold sweat and drag out your little black book
to hit up everyone you know for startup funds, let
me break down what I call the 'old world, new
world' realities when it comes to starting a business.

In the old world you needed cash and time to start a new company—you needed a physical location, at least an office or an office building and, in some cases, a warehouse and factory floor. You needed employees, goods, and packaging. Shipping, postage, and expensive marketing. In the old world, you were so deep in debt when you opened the door to your new company it took years, maybe a lifetime, to realize a profit.

Welcome to the new world—and that means starting a business online!

Today, you can get webhosting for five bucks a month, install a website to represent your business in a couple of hours, and get your first paying customers immediately (also in less than a few hours). I know it sounds impossible, but this new mentality is changing the way people do business, and it opens a new world for those who want to start a new business.

What about you? Since you're still reading, I assume you're considering changing your lifestyle. Making such a change takes guts, commitment, and passion—so, to begin our journey into understanding what this new type of online business looks like, let's explore what an online business is, as well as what it isn't. I hope I help dispel some of your fears about striking out on your own—and, to do that, I need to get down and dirty about passive income businesses.

AN ONLINE BUSINESS *IS* . . .

- **A 'REAL' BUSINESS.** Many think just because something exists purely online—no brick and mortar store, no open or closed sign, no time clock—that it isn't really a business. But just ask Amazon.com or Zappos.com how real they feel about their unlimited success online.

- **LOW STARTUP, HIGH POTENTIAL.** The startup for many online businesses is low-to-no cost, while the potential is limited to your imagination.

- **LOW MAINTENANCE, HIGH RETURNS.** Once up and running, you can maintain most online businesses with little to no daily involvement while providing high returns on a consistent basis. In fact, this is the beauty of the lifestyle business—your time is your own, and you determine how many hours a day, week, or month you want to spend on your business.

AN ONLINE BUSINESS *ISN'T* . . .

- **A WAREHOUSE FULL OF INVENTORY.** The challenge of running a traditional, old-fashioned business was the necessity for a warehouse full of goods, manufacturing equipment, or physical inventory. From subscription services to drop shipping, most online companies require no warehouse and no inventory—or, very little.

- **A LIFETIME OF DEBT.** In the old world or traditional style of starting a business, you needed a hefty loan—or, significant outsider investment—to start a company. Typically, loans or investment funds were used to pay for a physical location, desks, and chairs for employees, Worker's Compensation and other insurance, as well as subscription or license fees for necessary software and other necessary items. Today's online companies, however, can be operated cheaply, remotely, and with outsourced employees who bring their own computers, software, and additional required services to the equation— no insurance or worker's comp required.

- **A BALL AND CHAIN.** Most traditional brick and mortar businesses require a lifetime of routine maintenance. Running a traditional startup company means years of blood, sweat, and tears to get it off the ground and become successful. It also means years of hard work and constant, on-site efforts to prove a profit. Today, you can start an online business over the weekend with a very minimal investment fee, and you can realize a profit during your first week of business.

Don't believe me?

Keep reading . . .

WHAT NOW? WHAT'S NEXT?
WHAT'S A 'LIFESTYLE' BUSINESS?

According to QFinance.com, the term 'lifestyle business' means:

A small business typically run by individuals who have a strong interest in the product or service offered. For example, handmade greeting cards, jewelry, antique dealing, or restoring. Such businesses tend to operate during hours that suit the owners, and generally provide them with a comfortable living.

Meanwhile, TheFreeDictionary.com defines it as:

A small business in which the owners are more eager to pursue interests that reflect their lifestyles than to make more than a comfortable living.

Finally, from YourDictionary.com:

A small commercial enterprise operated more for the owner's enjoyment and satisfaction than for the profit it earns.

All are somewhat correct, but they're disturbingly wrong, as well. These definitions, while technically valid, make a lifestyle business sound as if it's little more than a poorly paid hobby, since they all seem to indicate the owners are not interested in making money from it.

But, that's not my experience. Or, my lifestyle. So for the purposes of what I do, and how I operate, I think it's important that you understand my definition of a lifestyle business. It clearly defines what I want from life, how I live my life, and how I go about putting my life first and my job second.

The Rasmus Lindgren Dictionary:

A lifestyle business is *a business that supports your desired lifestyle.*

EXAMPLES OF LIFESTYLE BUSINESSES

If you think owning a lifestyle business means chucking it all in, sleeping in a tent down by the river, and selling your wares at the local flea market, think again. (Unless, of course, that's the lifestyle business you're seeking!) Again, it's what you want—here are some examples of successful lifestyle businesses that will show you the wide range of existing opportunities—all it takes is opening your eyes to them and thinking about your personal and professional future a bit differently:

FREELANCE EBOOK COVER DESIGNER

eBooks, Kindles, Nooks, and online eBook sellers are booming. Why not cash in on this wave by outsourcing your graphics design expertise in a niche field like eBook covers? From the comfort of your home, hotel room, coffee shop, or a remote island, you can use a graphic arts program on your laptop to create magical works of art for clients all over the world. Charge what you want, as often as you want.

Then again, why do the work yourself? If you really want to take a lifestyle business such as this to the next level, why do the work yourself? Why not hire someone cheaper to do this for you in, say, the Philippines or Eastern Europe? You collect the money and pay the person who is fulfilling the order (this is the business model I'm using in a couple of my businesses—sell a service, and outsource the entire production.)

CONSULTANT

You can consult with people throughout the world by taking whatever expertise you have, in any field, and help others succeed in that field. I've used this type of online lifestyle business to gain more freedom by charging higher hourly prices. This way, I work less often each year, and use that mobility and freedom of time to travel where I want, when I want. All freedom, however, isn't just free time— when I'm abroad and simply making polite conversation at a bar, restaurant, or party, I'll meet people who need my services.

COACH OR PROFESSIONAL SPEAKER

Many coaches, consultants, or professional speakers can also have a successful online program. In addition to billable hours, they can sell content such as eBooks, podcasts, audio books, white papers, and video workshops or classes. By maximizing your efforts, you can turn a dream job into a lifestyle business! The more online content you have available, the less hands-on coaching you'll do, because it provides freedom of time and mobility. That translates into your going where you want, when you want, and for as long as you want! Eventually, you may evolve from being a hands-on consultant/coach to being an author, speaker, or thought leader—people simply click and download rather than meet and greet.

YOUR OWN DROP-SHIP COMPANY

Drop shipping means you don't carry inventory, but your supplier (typically the producer or a distributor) fulfills the order, and sends the goods directly to your customer. You earn a little less than if you have a warehouse of products yourself, but you have zero risk, and don't need a lot of money to invest in products. Zappos.com is a great example of a company that started with drop shipping and evolved into something else.

Perks or long-term goals of running a drop-ship company are the opportunities to sell it for a major profit. Many software companies begin this way, and they wind up selling for multiple times the start-up cost. It gives the owners plenty of money, time, and mobility to start other lifestyle businesses, or simply live their lifestyles.

There are lifestyle businesses for all lifestyles, incomes, and locations. Technology, talent, passion, skill, and the desire to change combine to ensure you find just the right lifestyle business for you!

YOU MIGHT BE A LIFESTYLE-BUSINESS ROCKSTAR!

Now you know the limitless horizons that await you—if you're searching for a business to suit your lifestyle, or a business that actually *is* your lifestyle—it's time to determine if it's the right life for you. Fair warning, I include this section because starting, owning, or joining a lifestyle business is not for everyone. Living the dream sounds easy, but if you're searching for a regular paycheck or the slow and steady, then you may want to consider other options.

The unwritten realities include the fact you're an independent contractor and often not an employee. You may be an employer. For those of us raised in the cubicles and catacombs of the typical corporate workplace, this can be a hard adjustment and, perhaps, a more difficult life. Then again, so can losing your job, being outsourced or downsized, or forced to work two jobs.

Clearly, steady employment and running your own lifestyle business have pros and cons—how do you feel about it? What are your strengths? Weaknesses? Tolerance levels? I believe there is a lower risk when you are your own boss. Think about it—at least *you* decide when to downsize or fire yourself! But . . . you don't have the luxury of working from nine to five. So, how do you feel about uncertainty, challenge, and hope?

Let's dig a little deeper . . .

YOU'RE TIRED OF THE DAILY GRIND

The very definition of a lifestyle business caters to those who want to live their lifestyles first and cater to their businesses second. If your job has taken over your life, you might want to reconsider putting your life before your work. I know—it's a concept that goes against everything you've been taught. But, in order to gain the most from the lifestyle business, you need to shed the old way of doing things. And, that can be scary. After all, when you head into the unknown, there's bound to be a bit of trepidation. However, if you never take a risk, then you'll be mired in the same old, same old . . . how rewarding is that?

YOU MISS YOUR FAMILY AND FRIENDS

Today's modern-paced businesses require forty-hour workweeks—however, fifty, sixty, or seventy-hour workweeks are the new norm. I'm not saying every lifestyle business rockstar only works four hours per week—what I am saying is working on your own terms is often the only way you're going to see your family and friends more than you are right now.

YOU'RE READY FOR A NEW CHALLENGE

Lifestyle business rockstars are ready for something new, unexpected, or challenging. What passions did you have when you were young? What did you want to accomplish? What did you want to do for a living? Fact is—it's easy to get lost in the rut of our daily jobs because we have to pay the bills first, and love what we do second. I speak to many individuals who tell me they lose sight of things because they have so much to do in order to make it through their regular routines. Think about that—no time for self or others.

Now, think about this . . .

YOU'RE NOT IMPRESSED WITH THE STUFF YOU BUY

Once upon a time, 'things' were important to me. I worked long and hard to be able to buy nice cars, clothes, and watches. I'd go out to eat every night, and entertain myself with all the toys, bells, and whistles. Starting a family, though, made me rethink my priorities—now I understand life is short, time is precious, and all those toys, things, and possessions pale in comparison to how I feel about the people in my life—and the time I get to spend with them each day.

What about you?

YOU'RE READY TO FIND THE RIGHT BALANCE BETWEEN MONEY, TIME, AND MOBILITY

There are three things that need to be in balance in our lives—money, time, and mobility. And yet, most of us live our lives out of balance. In an effort to make more money, we sacrifice time with our families, as well as the ability to be mobile. But, if we suddenly decide we want more time to do the things we love, it often means sacrificing money because we're taking precious hours away from work. Luckily, I have a solution! This book offers *The Rockstar Trifecta*—a solution to balancing money, time, and mobility so you decide what you need in order to achieve a work-life balance.

What it takes to be a lifestyle business rockstar has very little to do with your college degrees, how much you have in the bank, or whom you know. It's not even about what you know! It's more about what and whom you care about, as well as what you want to do with the rest of your life. Whether you're twenty, fifty, or eighty, it's never too early or too late to become a lifestyle business rockstar!

PARTING WORDS . . .
THE GREAT LIFESTYLE LIE

We can't change the past. We can't transport back to when our houses were worth more than we owed, when we made more than we spent, or when our credit cards weren't maxed out. What's worse, we can't undo the hurt, betrayal, or pain caused by the great lifestyle lie. Or, the disappointment.

We've grown up believing in something that isn't true—we've learned the hard way that security may give us peace of mind, but only until we realize we're the only security we'll ever need. The first step for creating a lifestyle business that fits *your* lifestyle is to believe it can happen.

It starts with you.

So far we've seen the problem, identified the solution, and gone so far as to test whether you're lifestyle business rockstar material. Now it's time to move forward and act on your dreams to change your life for the better.

Chapter Three
The Secret to Living Your Dream Life
The New World is Revealed in This Book!

"I do not believe a man can ever leave his business. He ought to think of it by day and dream of it by night."

~ Henry Ford

It's clear there is value in the old world and traditional way of doing business. However, if you want your dream of living a rockstar lifestyle to be a reality, the future is online. And not just online—but in an online, lifestyle business.

Really? How? How can you balance your money, time, and mobility and still make enough to support you and your family, to say nothing of living the lifestyle of your dreams?

I agree, it's a huge leap of faith, particularly if you've been fed the great lifestyle lie your entire life. But I'm here to tell you it can be done—all of it, if you'll just take that leap of faith and believe in yourself.

But it's more than just belief. It's a system. A process. In the coming sections of this book, I'm going to share tools to help you achieve your dream of starting and succeeding in your own lifestyle business.

THE ROCKSTAR TRIFECTA

Cornering the Market for Your Dreams

The cornerstone of this book is the *Rockstar Trifecta*, and it's your guide to achieving balance in your work and life. When I began my first lifestyle business, I did it for a variety of reasons—more money, more time with my family, and more mobility to travel as I please. I was dissatisfied with the old school—a nine-to-five world that wasn't giving me enough of the above. When the Rockstar Trifecta became clear to me, I realized why I began searching for alternatives to the old world business model—my life was lacking balance.

The Rockstar Trifecta offers you balance on a sliding scale. Need more time? Find a lifestyle business that provides it. Need more money? Find a lifestyle business that provides it. You get the idea. The Rockstar Trifecta will help determine how you can match your needs with a specific business that will provide more money in less time.

THE 4S MODEL OF LIFESTYLE BUSINESS DESIGN

Many people start a business while leaving out the most essential step—the design of that business. What will it look like? How will it feel, or fit into your daily life? How big will it need to be? Think about the type of business and lifestyle you want—how big or small? Will it scale? Or, will it grow without upsetting the apple cart?

It's vital you ask these questions before—not after—you start a business. With that in mind, I'll help you blueprint the design of your ultimate lifestyle business! It's always easier when you have someone in your corner and mentoring you for your success.

LIFESTYLE BUSINESS MODELING

You need to design your business before the first mouse-click you'll take to open it, so I'm taking the process further—in Part 4, I'll teach you how to design a business model, and I'll tie it in with the Rockstar Trifecta. For instance, if you want more time, you'll need to explore business models that allow for more time. The same goes for making more money—explore the business models that will allow you to do so.

After reading Part 4, you'll be better acquainted with the most common lifestyle business models, and you'll look forward to starting one or more of them on your own.

PARTING WORDS . . .
ACHIEVING YOUR LIFELONG DREAM

So far, you've learned you don't need a fortune to start your own business—it can be anything you want it to be, and if you model it correctly, you can have a true balance of money, time, and mobility to live the lifestyle you desire. Now comes the good part—you'll discover how the Rockstar Trifecta will change your life. And when you implement it, you'll find the lifestyle business of your dreams!

Part 2

The Rockstar Trifecta

Cornering the Market for Your Dreams

Chapter Four
Defining Balance

What is the Rockstar Trifecta?

"Try, try, try, and keep on trying is the rule that must be followed to become an expert in anything."
~ W. Clement Stone

Most of us have lived our own version of the stereotypical rockstar lifestyle at one point or another. With a big bonus, a little time off, or holiday, we go rockstar wild—champagne wishes and caviar dreams for as long as the good times last. Or, until the credit card bill comes in and we don't have enough to pay the interest, let alone the principle.

Maybe we do the opposite—we keep our noses to the grindstone and we rarely have time to see our family, let alone experience the opportunity to travel. We sacrifice for one corner of our lives, the monetary one, and we ignore the other two. Time and travel. We wake up to find ourselves old, grey, and sore. And our kids heading off for college!

But a life out of balance is not only unhealthy, it's straight up counterproductive to living. Ultimately, the Rockstar Trifecta is really about how to achieve the perfect, balanced life. Industry, company size, or skills don't matter—a life out of balance is a life heading sideways, not forward.

Again, this isn't about how to get rich—it's about how to live life on your own rockstar terms. That may mean living half of the year in a trailer in Florida, and the other in a tract house in Poughkeepsie. It may mean splitting your time between a villa in France, and a cottage in Malibu. It may mean working one day a week, or three days a week. Balance isn't about more or less—it's about feeding three of life's most basic needs.

Money. Time. Travel.

They're equal.

DEFINING THE ROCKSTAR TRIFECTA

First, let's define Rockstar Trifecta by breaking it down into two terms: a 'rockstar' is anyone who is living life on their own terms. That doesn't mean you have to wear leather pants and slap on two coats of eyeliner—it means if you're not technically your own life boss, you act like one. Second, a 'trifecta' is a balance of three critical factors that help craft the way you live. It's making the kind of money you find personally satisfying coupled with the kind of 'hanging around backstage' time you need to live well. The third component of the Rockstar Trifecta is the ability to travel—where, when, and for as long as you see fit.

In the coming sections, you'll learn what you need to know about each aspect of the Rockstar Trifecta, and you'll meet some extremely interesting people who live the Rockstar Trifecta. I know it's difficult to take my word for the Trifecta's success, so a few examples of such success are a good idea!

UNDERSTANDING THE ROCKSTAR TRIFECTA

Bottom line, the Rockstar Trifecta is all about helping people prioritize their lives. It's a simple, three-part formula you can use anytime or anywhere to help you assess how much your life is in balance. If it feels out of balance or out of control, you can make quick adjustments to reel in your life.

If you feel as if you don't have enough time, how can you achieve more time to yourself? If you don't have enough money, how can you make some while traveling? Or, instead of traveling?

I know these may sound like abstract questions to you, particularly if you're living in the nine-to-five grind. But I can almost guarantee if you're still in the corporate mentality and working nine to five, struggling from paycheck to paycheck, or working two jobs to pay your bills, your life is not in balance.

And it may never be.

The fact is it's likely you'll never fulfill your rockstar dreams of having your money, time, and mobility in balance if you continue to live by the nine-to-five mindset. You know—the mindset that places you in a cubicle or at a desk, onsite or in the office, every day, five days a week. The mindset that forces you to earn a salary. The mindset that ties you to a single company or employer. Since you're reading this book, I think you realize it's a dead end.

This book is about the open road, the unlimited horizon, and the endless journey. The types of companies I'll be listing will free you to create a business suited to your lifestyle, take advantage of the Rockstar Trifecta, and live your rockstar dreams!

Ask yourself this question—*if I didn't have to work, how would I balance my life as a rockstar?*

Where will I go? How will I live? How much time will I spend with family and friends?"

You'd be surprised by how often I hear the phrase, "But, Rasmus, I like my job. I really, really do!" Sure you do. So do I. I enjoy helping my clients, consulting with them, and improving their work lives and businesses. It's important to be productive and worthwhile, and that's how working makes you feel. Ask yourself these questions—*if I won the lottery tomorrow, would I still go to work? Would I spend my precious time hunched over a keyboard, clacking away, while another day passes in the average routine? And, another? And, another?*

A few people will say yes—typically, young men positioned at the beginning of their careers. But most say, *No, when you put it that way, I would quit my job and travel around the world . . .* or, *I would quit my job and write the great American novel . . .* or, *I would quit my job and spend my days at the beach . . ."* When you implement the Rockstar Trifecta, you'll begin to prioritize the 'I would'.

It boils down to this—your 'I would' revolves around money, time, or travel. Think about it. Can you think of anything you would do that doesn't connect to money, time, and travel?

Neither can I.

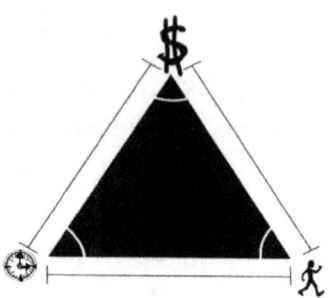

USING THE ROCKSTAR TRIFECTA
IN THREE STEPS OR LESS

In order to use the Rockstar Trifecta model and in order to live a balanced life, you must rid yourself of the nine-to-five mindset. I'm not saying quit your job today—but, start thinking about it. For this to completely work, you must accept there is another way to live your life without heading out to the office each day. Many find it difficult to accept. Many still prioritize money over time and travel.

Following are three steps to help you achieve your life balance by using the Rockstar Trifecta to its full advantage:

Step 1
Write Down all Current Expenses

You need to know where you are in order to decide how far you can go. I'm always amazed at the number of people I talk to who have no idea of their monthly expenses. Maybe their spouses take care of that stuff, or maybe they just pay bills as they come in, and they don't add it up as long as they have enough left over to dine out, catch a movie, or buy a new CD.

So, the first step to manifesting the Rockstar Trifecta is to write down all of your current expenses. It doesn't matter where you write it down—just do it! Once you know your expenses (not just your monthly bills, but also how many times you ate out that week, bought an iced coffee on the way to work, or how many books you downloaded for your Kindle), look at them with a critical eye. Which can you jettison away? Which are 'must haves' and 'could haves'? Which are luxuries you can do without while you transition to a rockstar lifestyle business?

I'm not suggesting you sell your house and start living below your current standard. By a certain point in our lives, we get used to a certain way of living—eating good food, sipping a glass of vintage wine, and enjoying ourselves within a certain budget. I don't want to be the one to tell you to start living like a student again!

It's important to get a rough idea of what kind of cash flow you need to bring in each month—minimum—in order to keep your current lifestyle. If you don't do that, you'll never get a handle on what you need to do in order to realize your personal rockstar lifestyle or how much you'll need to bring in each month to make it happen.

Step 2
Define How You Want to Spend Your Time

To value your time, it's important to understand how you'll spend your time. Is it an obscure hobby? Time with the family? Time for writing a book? Few of us consider what we might do with a little extra time—and the prospect of more time can make you feel like a kid in a candy store! If you're introverted, you may want to do stuff on your own and, if you're extroverted, you might want to spend time with others.

Step 2 is probably the hardest step in the process because we buy into the nine-to-five, play-on-the-weekends mindset.

Until the day we die.

Ask yourself questions such as, *What if it were the weekend all week long? How would that change my priorities?* Or, try to recall when you were a kid—you had dreams and goals! What would you do with your time if your job didn't require you to work forty, fifty, or sixty hours a week?

Step 3
Define What Places You Wish to See (and, with Whom)

If you had more freedom, where would you go? Who would go with you? Would you snowboard in the French Alps, or hang out with the family in a luxury bungalow by the sea? Where you go, and who goes with you has a lot to do with your rockstar lifestyle business.

Here's a tip—don't plan this step as if it's a vacation. This is a bucket list we're talking about—places you want to go. Ask yourself—*is this something I want to do for several months? Or, is it something I want to continue to do each year? Or, do I want to do or see something new each year?*

Chapter Five
The First Corner—CASH!

*"Money won't make you happy . . . but
everybody wants to find out for themselves."*
~ Zig Ziglar

I discovered early in my music producer career that most rockstars are shrewd businesspeople. I'm constantly amazed by how the rockstars of old keep reinventing themselves long after they can no longer fit into spandex, or have lost all of their hair. Especially in this digital age!

Gene Simmons is a great example—he reinvented himself numerous times throughout the years, most recently as the star of his own reality show. His show prominently features other businesses he set up for himself after Kiss.

Jonathan Cain, keyboardist and songwriter for Journey (arguably one of the most iconic rock bands of all time) reinvented himself as a solo smooth jazz artist. He has a string of pop albums which is a different genre than his earlier rock origins.

Reinvention occurs when rock music fades away, bands break up, or radio stations dissipate from the airwaves. Reinvention occurs when record sales plummet, age takes over, or listeners' tastes change. But for those who want to continue living the rockstar lifestyle without fading into obscurity, it's important to keep your mind on the money, and the money on your mind.

Period.

MONEY MATTERS, BUT NOT AS MUCH AS YOU MAY THINK!

You know money matters. Yes, to some more than others, but it still matters. In modern life, money is the number one indicator of how we live our lives. Usually, two working parents (some even have two jobs) slave in order bring in cash while the kids are in daycare. When we want a raise, we work harder and more for the promotion that might just buy an extra-bedroom house. But, people tend to focus only on money—and that's a problem. What you'll find as we go into more depth about the Rockstar Trifecta is you don't really need the money you think you need in order to snag more time and mobility. We save our entire lives, and then retire to have time and mobility—but by the time retirement rolls around, we have two false hips and inflation has eaten away most of our savings!

The beauty of the Rockstar Trifecta is that it's completely your own design. You decide how much money is enough to support your lifestyle, and it doesn't have to be in the millions of dollars to make you and your family happy. For some, it could be five figures, for others, eight.

What you want to decide before taking any plunge, quitting any job, or starting any company is how much money you need to live the lifestyle you want.

It's amazing how little money you might actually need once the physical trappings of your current life are on the table. When you think in terms of the Rockstar Trifecta and not the daily nine-to-five grind, things such as freedom, time with family and friends, and going to new places become more critical than the pricey jet ski, opening another credit card, or going all out for your second honeymoon.

When living your life becomes a priority over making a living, you'll realize what you don't need.

Imagine packing a few bags and just heading out on a grand adventure! Imagine learning a new language while you're in a new country, dining twice a week for dinner at places tourists only dream of, or exploring places only the locals know. Imagine having time for quiet dinners, a cold beer with old friends, or a hot toddy with new ones. Imagine looking forward to work that makes you happy, rather than dreading the job that pays the bills. If you have a burning desire to live a different lifestyle, live in a different country, and still enjoy a bright future, then these are the tools you'll need to make that happen.

And it may not cost as much as you think!

Many people say they could never afford to live in another country—yet, I'm not a millionaire, and I live in two! I always tell clients it's as easy to pay bills in Thailand as it is in Denmark, New York, or Paris. You'd be amazed at where people live, make an honest living, and live their adventures in this world!

Remember—prices go up and down, and you can rent or own a big or small place. It can be a little country farm, big city apartment, or a castle in Ireland. Also remember it's *your* dream . . . you *can* make the most of it!

Also remember the fact of geo arbitrage—this way you can make your money in dollars, but spend them in Thai Bath. You can live like royalty in a country such as Thailand while earning what would not be defined elsewhere as a big paycheck. You'll never know until you try and, take it from me—it isn't as expensive as you might think to live wherever you desire. It only takes research, forethought, planning and, of course, money.

It's important to remember money is one corner of the Rockstar Trifecta, and its main role is to fund the time you get to hang out backstage and travel wherever your rockstar dreams take you.

What follows is the story of one man who fused his lifestyle with his passion, and created a career unlike anything he could have imagined—complete with money, time, and mobility . . . as you read, keep in mind there isn't anything different about this guy—he could be you!

JOHNNY CUPCAKES

When a Rockstar Lifestyle Makes a Great Lifestyle Business

This story represents a true merging of a rock 'n roll lifestyle with a lifestyle business. In the early 2000s, a young man named Johnny Earle worked part-time at a local music store in Braintree, Massachusetts. He also played in a band and, being the creative type, he often designed the band members' performance shirts.

Fellow music-store staff nicknamed Johnny 'Johnny Cupcakes' and they began wearing the shirts on and off stage. The shirts featured a cupcake in the center of the design, and people responded positively to the design originality. Coworkers, band mates and store customers, as well as fans off the street asked where they could buy the T-shirts. It wasn't long until Johnny sensed a demand, and he ran more print runs of each design, selling them out of the back of his car. And, while touring with his band, Johnny took more shirts on the road to give away to band mates and other bands—eventually, demand grew for the comfortable shirts with their offbeat design.

A brand and lifestyle businesses were born.

Physical stores were at the heart of Johnny's personal branding message—today, however, Johnny Cupcakes is a virtual empire, and it includes a 24/7 online store that features T-shirts, and everything from boxers to jewelry. Johnny also lectures worldwide on entrepreneurism and business ownership, and he recently made *BusinessWeek* magazine's "Best Entrepreneurs 25 and Under" list.

Today, Johnny is the master of his own domain. He lives his rockstar lifestyle, hawks his wares from anywhere in the world, and he remains true to his entrepreneurial spirit—he always finds opportunity wherever he lands.

The bottom line is this—there isn't any reason you can't achieve the same rockstar lifestyle success as Johnny Cupcakes.

Be willing to learn and understand.

CASH IS KING—
PAYCHECKS ARE FOR PAUPERS

Cash is king and paychecks are for paupers. Take it from Johnny Cupcakes, who had this to say on his own website:

"When I was growing up, I'd always notice my mom being stressed/bummed out about her 9-5 job. Ever since, I've been coming up with little ways to work for myself."[2]

If you've come this far, you know my philosophy about jobs—the only lifestyle they're good for is the CEO's. If you want to live your lifestyle and not have your lifestyle work you to death, you have to be in business for yourself. The problem for most people, however, is fear. We're brainwashed by the great lifestyle lie to the point we fear trying to branch out for ourselves, let alone dream of succeeding.

In this book, you'll learn ways to start online businesses for little-to-no-money down. The low overhead reality of today's online business opportunities means you no longer have excuses for branching out on your own and acquiring the cash you need to live the lifestyle you desire.

---

[2] www.johnnycupcakes.com

I challenge you to keep your eyes, ears, and mind open to the opportunities this book presents. It's not about getting rich quick—it's about being wise to the real opportunities for success that abound for you with little money down. Keep reading, keep nodding your head, and keep believing in yourself. Carefully plan for a future of your dreams that is different from your current reality.

The biggest tragedy? Giving up. If you read this book, believe in what I'm telling you, and make grandiose plans—then you'll be on the path to living the rockstar lifestyle. You may not think so now, and you may be skeptical. However, I'm proof my method works—don't be afraid to dream big. And, don't give up! All giving up does is teach or reinforce quitting, and I think both of us know we'll never get anywhere if we operate with the mindset of quitting when the going gets rough.

PARTING WORDS . . .
CASH MONEY

Money is necessary, but it doesn't have to be a necessary evil. In the next two sections we'll discuss time and travel, and you'll realize when you open your mind to both, you can make them happen with whatever amount of money you make.

Remember, too, the Rockstar Trifecta is all about balance. Worrying too much about money or spending too much of it will quickly put your life and Trifecta out of balance.

In the nine-to-five world, money is a constant source of worry. When you focus more on time and travel, as well as the money you'll need to fulfill your life's goals instead of merely covering your monthly bills, money is clearly seen as a tool instead of a burden.

So. Moving forward. Rather than thinking of ways to make more money, think of ways to use the money you already make—it will fund your desired lifestyle and future!

Chapter Six
The Second Corner—TIME!

"You take on the responsibility for making your dream a reality."

~ Les Brown

The love and pursuit of money is ingrained in most of us and it's often the first thing we think about when making a life or lifestyle decision—so it makes sense that cash is the first corner of the Rockstar Trifecta. But for an increasing number of people, time is the freedom they crave. As with many things in life, we crave what we can't have. Or, what we think we can't have. Switch up your thinking a bit!

TIME IS OF THE ESSENCE

Work. Carpool. Shopping. Wait! I'm not done—your son's soccer game, your daughter's piano lessons, and a dentist appointment for you!

Today's employees work about fifty hours a week—and, when coupled with hours for a daily commute and a personal life, there's little free time left.

THE AVERAGE WORKDAY

Sound Familiar?

7:00 A.M. Up with the alarm. Shower, wake the kids up, get them ready for school.

8:00 A.M. Drop the kids off, or get them ready for the bus. Begin daily commute to work.

9:00 A.M. Arrive at work. Play catch up for what you neglected to finish yesterday.

10:00 A.M. Begin slogging through emails and voicemails. Organize and start your day.

11:00 A.M. First conference call or meeting of the day.

12:00 P.M. Lunch.

1:00 P.M. Back to work

2:00 P.M. Second meeting/conference call of the day.

3:00 P.M. Back to work.

4:00 P.M. Third and final meeting/conference call of the day.

5:00 P.M. Finish work.

6:00 P.M. Run errands on the way home from work.

7:00 P.M. Start dinner.

8:00 P.M. Eat dinner.

9:00 P.M. Get kids ready for bed, check homework, read a bedtime story.

10:00 P.M. Wind down with your spouse. Watch TV, read a book, listen to music.

11:00 P.M. Hit the sack, and get ready to start again.

Nothing special, right? Keep in mind it doesn't include random dates, deadlines, or special projects that keep you late at work. It doesn't include a major holiday recital, birthday, or field trip. So when you add personal time, you can see how your time can spiral out of control.

And this is the schedule for years. Why?

Money.

And, fear. We're scared we'll lose our jobs. Did you notice in the sample schedule 'free time' isn't mentioned once?

THE ROCKSTAR TRIFECTA SCHEDULE

Here's an example of my rockstar lifestyle:

7:00 A.M. Wake up before the family for a quick swim in the pool.

8:00 A.M. Wake the kids up and have breakfast together.

9:00 A.M. Walk to the beach as a family, and watch the kids play.

10:00 A.M. Head back home and field a quick conference call.

11:00 A.M. Filming a video to post online for my Private Mastermind Group.

12:00 P.M. Lunch downtown at a new place we've never tried.

1:00 P.M. Shop for dinner as we walk back home.

2:00 P.M. Quick Skype call with a new strategic partner.

3:00 P.M. Update the blog.

4:00 P.M. Play date in the park with our neighbors.

5:00 P.M. Coffee/tea at a corner café.

6:00 P.M. Back home for dinner.

7:00 P.M. Play with kids.

8:00 P.M. Kids to bed.

9:00 P.M. Relax with a cold beer.

10:00 P.M. Attend an online course in SEO

(Search Engine Optimization) to add another facet to my consulting portfolio.

11:00 P.M. Netflix—a movie before bed.

My schedule isn't extreme—it's a snapshot of one family enjoying the Rockstar Trifecta. I haven't made anything up, and it's how we live our lives, enjoy our lives, and look forward to the rest of our lives.

THE GIFT(S) OF TIME

Take it from me—time with my family during the last few years is precious to me. Watching my children grow—not just at night or on the weekends—is something I wouldn't have been able to enjoy if I'd been a part of the workday grind. Life is my choice—I can wake up early to get a jump on the day, or I can sleep in. I schedule my time— Skype calls, workshops, or meetings. Of course, I have responsibilities, but the difference is I have the time to juggle and prioritize them, and everything is according to my plans.

Time is a lifestyle business rockstar dream and luxury—for instance, my girlfriend is on extended leave from her job because she wants to be close to the kids while they are small. If we didn't live the rockstar lifestyle, she wouldn't have the opportunity to create and enjoy such memories.

So while most people go back to work after six-to-ten months of maternity leave, my girlfriend is still home. I confess, we did have two kids back-to back—but only because we had the opportunity and we didn't need the money. I'm grateful our lifestyle business also fits our lifestyle, and affords us the opportunity to enjoy our lives.

Here are more gifts of time you'll experience when you openly embrace and engage in the Rockstar Trifecta: mental and physical health, travel, quiet, little, and big moments. Family moments. Coaching your kids' sports team. Family togetherness. You probably know there are many more perks—they'll depend on what you want out of your life!

Even if there weren't perks outside of providing the opportunity for more time, money, and mobility, an online business is still worth considering!

PARTING WORDS . . .
TIME

Time is finite—all of us have the same twenty-four hours a day and, depending on a host of factors such as genetics, health, and diet we're around for eighty to ninety years.

The Second Corner—TIME!

Do you really want to spend your time working for someone else, laboring under the false impression that your time is as valuable to them as it is to you? Instead, why not take back your time and spend it on yourself? Do what you want to do. Go where you want to go. Enjoy life.

Interested? Check out the last corner of the Rockstar Trifecta . . .

Chapter Seven
The Third Corner—MOBILITY!

"Success is not the key to happiness. Happiness is the key to success. If you love what you are doing, you will be successful."
~ Albert Schweitzer

Most of us regard travel as something we do on vacation. If you live the Rockstar Trifecta, however, mobility isn't something you earn at work. It's a daily lifestyle—an habitual behavior—that allows you to explore your world. Wherever and whenever.

The Third Corner—MOBILITY!

Do you realize most people rarely leave their hometown or state during the year? Some never leave! Danes usually travel by charter—we book one or two weeks each year that is someplace warmer than Denmark. We use one or two tropical weeks to help us recharge our batteries for the rest of the year after our return. Some travel more during the year (most people have five or six weeks of holiday each year), but the trips are usually one or two weeks at a time. The problem with this type of travel is that your body only starts to relax after a few weeks, and then it's right back to work. When it comes to living a different type of lifestyle, wouldn't you rather spend one-to-three months somewhere else?

While it's true you may have no interest in visiting Thailand, Denmark, or Russia there must be someplace you've always wanted to go. Even if it's going to the beach, restaurants you've always heard about one town over, or to a museum three states away. If your current lifestyle isn't making your dream a reality, then, indeed, there is something out of whack with your current lifestyle.

I'm not kidding. If you don't have the time, the money, or the energy to go someplace right now that you've always wanted to go, then you are simply not free. No exaggeration.

Now, I'm going to show you why.

Meet Yamile Yemoonyah . . .

In May of 2011, Yamile decided she wanted to see the world—you know—take a trip or two. But as she traveled more, Yamile realized there was nothing tying her down to any one place. Adopted in Columbia and raised in Germany, she had always had an international flair about her and, true to her roots, Yamile decided to continue her personal and professional journey. For the last year, she hasn't had a permanent, physical address. She relies on a friend's address in her hometown of Berlin for the few pieces of physical mail she receives, and she's exploring incorporating her business in the British Virgin Islands—no taxes, and she already has a bank account there.

This past year, she traveled to Spain, Majorca, Portugal, France, Holland, and Belgium—and that's just for a start! She generally stays a few months in each spot, and recently traveled to the States—Asia and Thailand are next. Describing herself as a slow traveler, she prefers to spend months instead of days in an effort to enjoy the people and culture, as well as to absorb the lifestyle.

But how can Yamile support her ex-pat lifestyle?

She opened Creative Web Biz.

Creative Web Biz is an online support center for various creative people, and she sets up online shops to sell her clients' creations or creative services.

In addition to setting up a web page, Yamile helps drive traffic to the site by working with her clients on SEO strategies, social media, and other marketing and promotional efforts. By helping others with her proven expertise, Yamile works from anywhere, and she does her one-on-one coaching via Skype. She does the work on her computer.

Yamile established a name by working with creative folks who could benefit from a website— artists, writers, and cooks. Probably more. As long as there is a need, she fills the niche!

She credits her expertise in web design while selling her own art online. At first, without the money to hire a web designer, she researched it and began designing her own. Now, by choice, Yamile works a little each day, up to four hours. She might work for a few hours first thing in the morning, and then head out for lunch, visit a few sites, or meet friends for an early dinner. Then she might work another hour or two in the evenings.

She can work anywhere, and truly runs her business from her laptop. While she always makes sure to stay in a place with an internet connection, she can work in a crowded café, a library, or a cozy corner.

The main tools of Yamile's trade are free online options that include things like Gmail, WordPress (for blogging and designing websites for her clients and herself), as well as Skype to communicate with

clients and others—none require a bunch of cash to stay in business.

Yamile uses WordPress because it provides an easy hand off when it comes time for her clients to be more independent and make updates for themselves. Her goal isn't to provide support for life, but, instead, to provide her clients the tools they need to empower themselves to manage, maintain and update their own sites.

For the future, Yamile looks forward to writing and filming more courses to help her clients find independence—and to gain more passive income.

While she enjoys her work, the online courses help drive passive income and fund her future endeavors which include taking a four-week survival course in the desert, and visiting the Amazon. Neither have great internet connections!

PARTING WORDS . . .
MOBILITY

Yamile isn't a superhero. She doesn't come from money, she's not a millionaire or a trust-fund baby, and yet she's living her life freely, passionately, and creatively.

She travels light. When we spoke about the best brands of luggage for frequent travelers, she quite bluntly stated that she uses a backpack. Period. She's a modern and content digital nomad, helping others create while living the rockstar lifestyle on her own terms. Her tools are technical, but not blazingly high-tech or so exclusive that they're not readily available to anyone, anywhere in the world. So, if you feel as if you need to have the best computer, the best phone, and the best of everything in order to create an online business, ditch that thought and remember Yamile. She can operate her business from anywhere in the world with a backpack and a laptop. She has more freedom than most people I know, regardless of their income.

Inspiring, isn't she?

PART 3

The 4S Model of Lifestyle Business Design

Chapter Eight
Why You Need Your Own Business

"A business is a repeatable process that makes money. Everything else is a hobby."

~ Paul Freet

So, why do you need to start your own business? Isn't it easier to keep your job and the status quo? Is it easier to go the independent route? Maybe. It may seem as if being independent is the easiest entrée into the lifestyle business rockstar dream— but, the fact is you can spend less money on taxes if you are considered a business. In fact, I have three very good, unarguable reasons why you should start your own business:

REASON # 1

It's Cheaper!

As an individual or sole proprietor, you pay taxes on all income. As a business entity, you only pay taxes on profits. This means all the materials, supplies, and additional essentials you buy for the company are paid *before* taxes.

In Denmark, we have high income taxes—we pay approximately 50% income tax and, over a certain limit, we pay a 'top tax' which means everything above that is taxed approximately at 70%. However, the corporate tax is only 25% on profits—you save more if you *own* a business instead of work *for* a business. Of course, tax rates vary according to locale, but you get the idea.

Another thing to keep in mind is tax structures change—have you ever seen the amount of paper that goes into the Tax Code? Keep on top of changes and you'll be in good shape!

REASON # 2

You'll Never be a Lifestyle Business Rockstar Working Nine to Five

Working for an hourly paycheck makes a living, but it doesn't fund a rockstar lifestyle. Not only will you never get rich working for an hourly wage, you'll never have the time or mobility you need to live the life of your dreams.

Starting your own business, no matter how big or small, is your ticket to freedom. Remember, you don't gain personal freedom by living life as an employee. Yes, there are those who worked their ways up the ladder and made it to the top—are you one of them? Do you think you'll be one of them? Is it possible for you to be one of them?

All good questions.

Whether you need more money, time, or mobility, your own lifestyle business will provide the necessary flexibility to balance your Rockstar Trifecta. Flexibility is the key—can you imagine going to your boss to tell him or her you can't work that day because you have a boatload of errands to run? Holy cow! Your sanity would be in doubt, and it could wind up being your last day at work!

REASON # 3

You Want More from Life

The 'more' I'm talking about may not be financial, professional, or personal—maybe, for you, it's undefinable right now. But it's there— simmering under the surface. Since you're reading this book, I know you want more from life, and chances are good you want to live the rockstar lifestyle.

Designing a business to fit your needs will help you live the life you've always dreamed of, and on your terms. It won't happen overnight. It may take a year or two.

It will take effort.

It will be worth it.

DESIGNING YOUR LIFESTYLE BUSINESS
WITH THE 4S MODEL

Lifestyle business design—designing your business according to your lifestyle—offers personal freedom. Think about it—what do you need from the Rockstar Trifecta? Money? Time? Mobility? Whichever you need, you can start a business that works for you using the following 4S Model:

THE FIRST S

SIMPLE SETUP: A lifestyle business (versus a turnkey or franchise business) should be easy to setup with low overhead and easy access. (Low overhead means you don't need a lot of money or time to set it up.)

THE SECOND S

SMALL IN SIZE: Start small. Simple things are simple to manage. You probably won't make millions, but a $5,000 a month business is easier to manage (and, it requires less time) than a $1,000,000 a month business.

THE THIRD S

SCALING BUILT IN: Notice, in the Second S, I said 'start' small—that doesn't mean your business won't grow. As it grows, it needs to scale so it doesn't overwhelm you or your lifestyle. You need to design the business so it can scale (even without you).

THE FOURTH S

SECONDARY TO YOUR LIFE: Your lifestyle business should come before business. This is the most controversial of the 4S Model because people think a business's goal is to make as much money as possible. However, for many people, time and mobility are equally important. They want to have the flexibility to go where they want for an undetermined amount of time.

They want to be free.

Chapter Nine
The First S—SIMPLE SETUP

"Motivation is what gets you started. Habit is what keeps you going."
~ Jim Rohn

Look for a rockstar lifestyle business with a low overhead that is easy to setup. It should offer a low point of entry, and room to move. A lifestyle business should be easy to start, and quick to get you to work. It shouldn't require many resources (time and money) to get started. Remember, this is not an office building, research park, or warehouse. You shouldn't need hundreds of thousands of dollars' worth of venture capital, and you shouldn't have to spend years creating a business in order to be able to reap the benefits. You—*you*—most likely, are the only resource in the company and you need to do most of the work. You can, of course, find help by outsourcing needs such as building a website or starting a blog. I still recommend, though, you do most of the groundwork—you'll learn the skills you can later outsource.

Building a lifestyle business isn't about living a four-hour workweek—at least not right away. It does take hard work in the first few months. The idea is to build a fully operational business so it won't require much maintenance. I recommend building a business that won't take more than a few months to be operational—it will depend on how much you allot to it in additional to your regular nine-to-five gig.

For example, my business, http://getashop.dk, supplies small Danish companies with commerce solutions. I created it in one week using only sixty-five dollars—fifteen bucks for the design template, and fifty bucks for the logo created by a freelance graphic designer on Elance.com. That was then—today you can get a simple logo for only five dollars!

The first week consisted of writing the content for the website, and searching for a provider that could create the actual ecommerce sites. Ten days later, I had my first two clients for a profit of over $1,500 on a $65 investment. If I had rented an office, purchased or leased equipment, and hired two employees right away, I'd be paying them instead of myself. *A small setup fee virtually guarantees profits right away!*

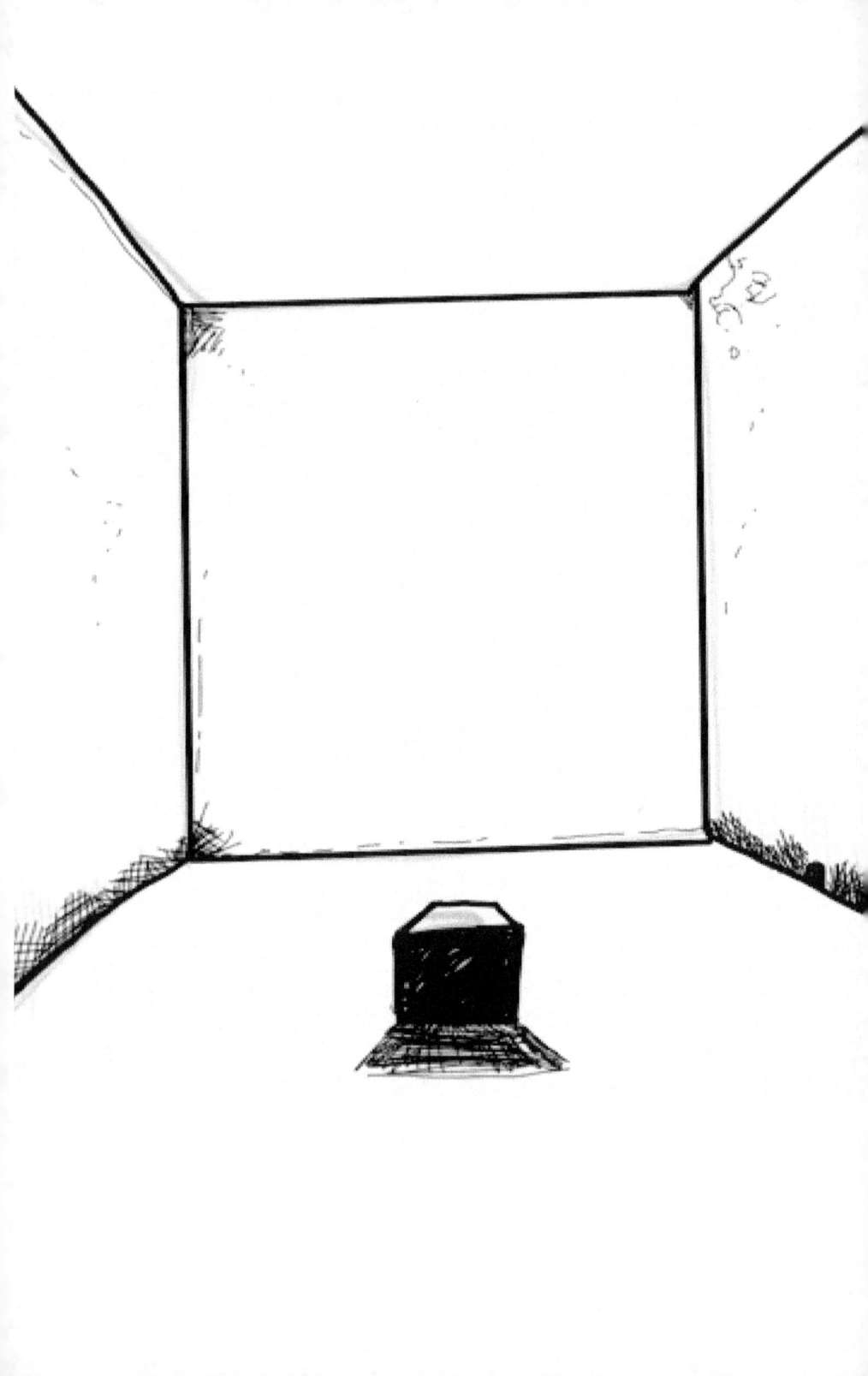

Chapter Ten
The Second S—SMALL IN SIZE

*"What the mind of man can conceive and
believe, it can achieve."*
~ Napoleon Hill

The Second S is for keeping it small—small and easy things are simple to manage. Make it something you can operate out of your extra bedroom, or something you can do at night or on weekends if you still need your nine-to-five job to make ends meet.

By now, you understand you're not going to make millions in the first year using the 4S strategy—so, how do you feel about $50,000? Does that amount enable you to leave your nine to five and be your own boss? Does it buy you the time you need to work fewer days or downsize to part-time so you can coach your kid's football games, wake up later, or travel more? Don't forget the new profits (balance) you realize when you adjust your life to the Rockstar Trifecta and 4S strategy!

It's prudent and wise to keep it simple—don't attempt to build the next Skype, Facebook, or Apple. For now. For your first time at bat, be ready to settle for a small, simple business that will supply you with a little extra cash and a lot more freedom. Once you find the business strategy that suits you, you can always start an additional rockstar lifestyle business because you aren't spending too much time on the first one! Multiple income streams are your friend and once you build your first business, you'll have the confidence, skill, and time to create a new one.

Remember the main goal isn't to become a millionaire or to get rich quick—it's to balance your life by finding the time and mobility you crave. If you create a successful lifestyle business and get it operating, then there is nothing holding you back from creating another one. This also helps with one of the questions I get from a lot of people—*Rasmus, I get all these ideas—which one should I choose?*

It doesn't matter. Select one to do first!

Unfortunately, many people never get past the idea phase. If you want to be ahead of the game, take action on one small, simple idea and you're already in the lead. Remember—it doesn't matter what idea you select because you can always select another after the first.

Start somewhere!

As Woody Allen once said regarding business— *eighty percent of success is showing up.*

Sometimes, though, things don't go as planned. If the first business you start isn't successful, you learned things you wouldn't have otherwise known. And, since we're stressing low effort and low start-up costs, you won't break the bank attempting to find the perfect lifestyle business for you. Remember—lifestyle businesses are easy to setup (the First S), so you can always create a new one if it doesn't work out the first time. True, you may lose a little time, but it's worth it if you gain valuable lifestyle business experience.

If your goal is a business with hundreds of employees funded by venture capital, then you should be prepared to work hard for years.

Really hard.

It's not for me—if I can't prove out my initial idea in a couple of months, I move on to something else and accept it didn't work.

Keep the businesses small, and the profits big!

Chapter Eleven
The Third S—SCALING BUILT IN

"If you are not willing to risk the unusual, you will have to settle for the ordinary."

~ Jim Rohn

When you sell your time for money (like in a nine-to-five job), you earn more if you work more. In a lifestyle business, you need to build something that can scale (grow with and adapt to your specific needs) so you can make more money without working more. This is a design goal, as well.

Although you can spend your time setting up the business, once it's operating your time shouldn't depend on the number of customers or clients you attract. Typically, some management is involved in the process, but if you were to graph your business success, your time spent on the business shouldn't be above income. If it is, you are selling your time again.

One of my businesses is www.backlinks.nu—it sells SEO (search engine optimization). Whether I have 1 or 100 clients, it still just takes me one-to-two hours per month to maintain this profitable site. All I have to do is log into the system, pull a report, and send the details to my production team. Then they'll fill the orders. Here's the beauty—I spend about two hours of my time if I have 100 clients, and about one hour if I have one client. Do you see that at 'x' amount of clients per hour, it scales well?

Did you notice I said 'production team'? In the beginning, you can accept to do the actual work per client if you like, but you should have a clear plan for how to outsource the work you're doing as your company grows and scales. If you end up with a complex product that only you can fulfill or produce, then you end up selling your hours again.

When considering scaling businesses, it's a good idea to keep the product simple. Start out with one product because you can always expand later. What's the rush? Anything is up for grabs—and, open for business when it comes to the online blank canvas.

It's a lot to think about, I know—feel free to scratch out some notes on the next page!

NOTES:

Chapter Twelve
The Fourth S—SECONDARY TO YOUR LIFE

"There is only one success—to be able to spend your life in your own way."

~ Christopher Morley

I believe a lifestyle business should be something secondary (the Fourth S) to your ultimate goals which lie in the Rockstar Trifecta. Your business can be something you are passionate about—passion helps you to focus, but remember the business should be secondary to your life goals.

The Fourth S should support your main goal in life, so remember the lifestyle business definition—lifestyle first, business second.

According to my colleagues, my stance is controversial. I talked with one guy who runs a media print house—he used to work seventy-hour weeks until he was diagnosed with a severe disease. Obviously, not good! Even though he has a wife and children, he still believes the right way to be a proper entrepreneur is to work seventy hours.

Even if it kills him.

Your life comes first, and it will feel great to create something. Remember, however, you also have goals that involve your family, personal development, and traveling. And if you don't—then it really is all about you and your rockstar lifestyle!

PART 4
Lifestyle Business Modeling

Chapter Thirteen
Six Benefits of
Starting an Online Business

"The way to get started is to quit talking and begin doing."

~ Walt Disney

Before we delve into actual business modeling, I want to discuss the differences between online businesses and brick and mortar businesses—you may know them, but I'll recap to be sure.

5 THINGS AN ONLINE BUSINESS ISN'T . . .

- **A FAKE BUSINESS.** Online businesses are real, valid, useful, and profitable.

- **A HOBBY.** Sure, you can set it and forget it in most online businesses, but only after you're ready to hand off your responsibilities to someone else.
- **A SCAM.** Are Amazon, Angie's List, and Zappos scams? All are online businesses which prove the internet is simply another storefront for today's busy, global customers.
- **HERE TODAY, GONE TOMORROW.** True, the internet is littered with dead websites, broken dreams, and business ventures doomed to failure. That's because many people take to the internet in search of overnight millions rather than focusing on a solid plan.
- **SPAM.** I'm not talking about the type of business that litters your inbox with offers that are too good to be true. Your online business will be honest and respected. Great business people know honesty and respect are important for a successful business—without them, your chances of maintaining success are diminished—a lot.

5 THINGS AN ONLINE BUSINESS IS . . .

- **SIMPLE.** Online businesses are simple to start and easy to maintain.
- **FAST.** Many online businesses can be started much faster than a brick and mortar business!

- **PROFITABLE.** For low startup and lower maintenance (see below), you can earn a steady profit and eventually support your family.
- **LOW OVERHEAD.** Remember my starting my business for only sixty-five dollars? I'm proof it can be done, and I'm no different than you!
- **LOW MAINTENANCE.** With minimal effort and upkeep, your online business can run smoothly and profitably for as long as you wish to keep it.

As you were reading through the five things an online business is, did you realize they are identical to those for starting any lifestyle business? Do you realize that starting an online lifestyle business doubles the benefits with half the effort? When you follow my lead by considering what an online business is and isn't, I'm confident you'll find the online business that is best for you. What works for you may not work for someone else, and vice versa—figure out what will work for you and your lifestyle.

SIX BENEFITS OF STARTING AN
ONLINE BUSINESS

Check out how online businesses compare with their brick and mortar counterparts:

BENEFIT #1

Immediacy

You can start an online business in one day, and certainly in one weekend. Your work involves setting up and personalizing a basic template storefront, and modifying it as you gain experience, products, or services. An idea on Friday can be a business by Saturday. Try doing that in a brick and mortar setting!

BENEFIT #2

Every day. Every minute. Every second.

Online businesses are always operating, and they can take orders twenty-four hours a day. While some choose to handle fulfillment by themselves, if they outsource they can fulfill orders day *and* night.

Even service industries can operate non-stop. While I take Skype calls or meetings during regular hours, I also have online workshops, tutorials, and video blog posts to keep the passive income rolling in. Try selling socks at midnight, or taping a seminar at five in the morning before going back to sleep or for a jog on the beach.

If you're an adult reading this book then likely your parents lived and breathed this mentality—go to school, get an education, and a good job. Buy a house, start a family, and keep working. Forget you only had two weeks off in the summer and a winter holiday. Forget it took you thirty years to own your home. Forget—well, I could go on about how the traditional way of beginning a business begets nothing but hard work.

And more hard work.

Think about it—the online world may seem too easy because you learned to work too hard.

BENEFIT #3

Simplicity

When I speak to people about starting an online business, they often tell me technology intimidates them. I understand their complaint, but from our cell phones to our webcams, website templates, and online storefronts, everything is plug-and-play today.

It's a lame excuse.

I remember when I started my blog—it was 'pick a design and start adding features' site. Want a link for followers? Click a button and add it. Want a traffic counter? Add one. Uploading a graphic? Just grab it from your desktop, and it will automatically shrink to fit. Want to upload a ton of posts but not post them until next week or next month? The system will automate it for you. And, the web cam in my MacBook works as a video camera, a still camera, *and* a microphone. I plugged it in, and a series of screens and windows on my desktop walked me through the process. Programs such as Skype are easy to use— you visit the website, click a link, and it will download, start running, and walk you through setting up a profile and making your first test call.

The internet is practically begging you to make money!

BENEFIT #4

Low Maintenance

Not only is today's technology begging you to join the online business culture, it also makes your site easy to maintain, automate, and promote. No matter what you're trying to do—ship an order, receive an order, or publish a blog post—there is likely a way to automate it.

Let's say it's close to the holidays—you can spend your four hours this week designing a holiday logo and writing all six posts to get you through December. If you feel like it, you can write the blog posts in the summer, and they'll appear on the dates you designate.

One of the coolest things about an online business? As long as you have WiFi and a laptop, you are free to operate your business from anywhere!

Check out the brick and mortar store—it's a fulltime, every day gig. You put up your seasonal products and displays to correlate with the seasons. Maybe you design them early, but there's no automation involved—you have to be there making it happen. Windows need washing, staff needs pampering, and inventory needs to be unloaded and stocked. Even in service industries, there is an office to maintain, calls to take, and appointments to make.

The list continues, ad nauseam . . .

I'm thinking you're recognizing the difference between the two. When you begin to add up all of the various things that will cost you money, you may want to consider rethinking the brick and mortar business model. A lifestyle business is so much easier! Cheaper, too!

BENEFIT #5

Passive

Benefits #4 and #5 are partners—you automate your systems and delivery, blog posts, and updates. By implementing careful planning and forethought, you can operate your online business efficiently, passively, and with low maintenance! Online businesses can be automated, and it makes them perfect vehicles for passive income. Remember, however, it must be designed properly from the beginning. If you don't take the time to design your online business properly, it will show in the outcome and results of your business. Not having enough time becomes an excuse, albeit a lame one. If you feel you don't have enough time to create your online business, then you should make time!

BENEFIT #6
Freedom

While your online business is operating passively, you're free to do as you please. Work more, play more, or travel more. A passive source of income means you can start an online business while employed full-time, gradually earning more from your online business. Or, you can start a second internet business. You're free to grow as fast or slow, big or as small as you wish!

That's the thing about freedom—without it, you'll never live the life of your dreams. With it, you can maximize your potential in anything you wish. To achieve your freedom, all you have to dream— and then make it happen by making changes.

HOW ONLINE BUSINESSES FIT IN THE 4S MODEL

Previously, I discussed the 4S Model that indicates the characteristics of a good lifestyle business. Now, how do you take the next step?

A few years ago it would have been nearly impossible for the average person to create a lifestyle business without needing tens of thousands of dollars. While the internet is no longer anything entirely new, the true innovation is *accessibility of technology*. It's easier to create a website, accept payments, and send invoices because of the plug-and-play technology that now dominates the entrepreneurial landscape. You no longer need to be a computer geek or have your sixteen-year-old nephew help you create an online business. The fact is if you can point and click a computer mouse, then you can create your online business from scratch.

Yourself. No help from anyone. Solo.

Online businesses give you much more freedom, and they live up to the characteristics of lifestyle business defined in the 4S Model. Let's look at how the traits of an online business fit with the 4S Model of running a lifestyle business:

THE FIRST S

Simple Setup

A lifestyle business should be easy to setup—I can show anybody without prior experience how to create a professionally designed website with a PayPal payment button in less than one hour.

How's that for an easy setup? This is what I mean when I say technology is accessible for the average consumer. Today's software and hardware manufacturers are eager for everyone to use their products because they doubled—tripled—tested them to make certain every fourth grader in the world can use them!

Yes—you can do it.

For example, most web hosting companies have what's called a '1 click install' format—it allows you to install a number of website building systems (also known as Content Management Systems, or CMS) with a click of the mouse. No need to know about codes, HTML, or anything more complicated than choosing the design of your website, and how to click, pull, or drag items on the webpage template.

These types of software are 'open source' and free. Systems such as WordPress (which currently powers more than fifty million websites online), make it easier than ever to start an online business in an afternoon. Or, a day. Or, a weekend.

The internet houses 'software as a service', or SAAS applications. That means they run everything—all you have to do is sign up and pay a small monthly fee. SAAS applications, such as Shopify.com, can have your new ecommerce site running in no time at all, making your online business easy to setup and automate.

THE SECOND S
Small in Size

A lifestyle business should be small. When you can start a website with so little effort it suddenly also becomes viable to create smaller businesses than before. This is why you're seeing niche sites—a site where the owner is targeting a very small niche. A niche that would have been unprofitable had it not been for the internet and its ability to target the world.

THE THIRD S
Scaling Built In

An online business is easier to scale (grow) than a brick and mortar company. When we talk about an online business, we talk about technology—and technology is good at automation. For instance, the process of taking an order, sending the notification to the warehouse, and sending an invoice to the customer can be done in a second, and without any human involvement.

Online businesses can be operated from anywhere as long as you have an internet connection. It's also a prime candidate for hiring people in low salary countries, and outsourcing various business functions such as customer support and order fulfillment.

Automation. Simplicity. Passive income. All define a lifestyle business and an online business. When you learn how to take advantage of the technology tools, you augment your chances of operating a successful online business. Knowing when to pass your duties to someone else is key, and you'll be ready to let go and enjoy your lifestyle business!

THE FOURTH S
Secondary to Your Life

It's easy to create an online business that's secondary to your lifestyle. Instead of a huge loan from the bank for a brick and mortar business, you can relax more and choose your battles. In other words, you can choose for yourself when and where you want to work on your business. When you achieve that you achieve being in control of your own life. You can go anywhere, anytime, with anyone. When you think about it, does it get any better than that? I don't think so.

PARTING WORDS . . .
STARTING AN ONLINE BUSINESS

If there were still an argument against opening an online business, I hope this chapter has put it to rest. Obviously, every case will be different and every business is unique—I hope I dispelled your fears, reservations, and concerns.

Online businesses are simple, fast, and easy. The have low overhead, and they generate passive income.

They're the present and the future.

In the following chapters, I'll walk you through a variety of online business models which are designed with automation in mind. Once you start them, you can quickly and easily hand them off to ensure that your time is exactly that—your time.

Chapter Fourteen
Lifestyle Business Modeling

"A goal is a dream with a deadline."

~ Napoleon Hill

Now—the guts of the matter! You understand how wonderful owning a lifestyle business can be, how much money, time, and mobility it can offer you, and how online is the way to go. You learned how any business, online or off, lifestyle or brick and mortar, should adhere to the 4S Model.

Now it's time for choices.

Which business model will be right for you? That's the ultimate question of this section, and for this book. My goal—for you to discover the variety of business models available online that follow the 4S Model—and it won't require a fortune to get started!

There is a variety of ways to make money online, and the following chapters represent a small fraction of the opportunities that exist for you. I'll discuss the four, basic business models that provide the most opportunity for the least amount of effort, as well as time, buy-in, and money.

Remember, these aren't just business models— they're also lifestyle business models. As we work through the following chapters, be thinking about what type of business is a good fit for you. Consider a style of working, living, and earning that clicks with you.

Don't seek out the business model that earns the most money, unless that's what you're seeking in your Lifestyle Trifecta. Search for a business model that you can start quickly, ramp up easily, and start earning gradually—over time you will create passive income. Think about it—passive income—come to grips with what that means, and think about how you can live your life and earn money while you sleep. What will you do differently? Will you take time to travel? Will you have more time to enjoy your family and friends?

Yes!

A FEW WORDS . . .
PASSIVE INCOME

I often get skeptical looks when I talk about passive income. Notice in all four of the business models I'll be discussing, they are businesses that require little maintenance once they are set up. You will work hard to get started, but it won't require a ton of consistent, daily follow through—you'll earn while-you-sleep money.

I'm not trying to sell you on some get-rich-quick scheme—that's the opposite of a lifestyle business. Passive income is no different from investing in a certain stock in 2011 and doing nothing with it for five years other than watching it grow. In whatever year you choose, you'll hopefully sell your stock for a profit.

That's it! Passive income. Money while you sleep.

The following four business models, however, provide more control over your money—you will choose the type of business, how much time you spend on it, and how many of these businesses you want to create. Don't forget you can have more than one lifestyle business—I know one woman who is planning on four within the next couple of years. She's planning all of them now . . .

As a quick way to figure out what's best for you, write down your passions, and then figure out what online business fits your passions best.

AUTOMATION—THE HEART OF THESE 4 BUSINESS MODELS

Automation creates passive income. If you can create a *set it and forget it* business such as a website or information product, by using technology and modern tools to automate systems of delivery, updating, and shipping you will be able to step away from the business and live your life. I'll repeat those last few words—*live your life.* Isn't that why you're reading this book? Aren't you looking for an alternative way of doing business other than the nine-to five? That's the point. Right?

The four, rockstar lifestyle business models are:

MODEL #1

Drop shipping

MODEL #2

Online services

MODEL #3

Affiliate marketing—little investment and time

MODEL #4

Informational products—sell knowledge

One of the online business may work for you— or, all of them may work! Remember to start small, and grow as you gain experience.

PARTING WORDS . . .
FOUR BUSINESS MODELS

There is a variety of business models from which to choose—these samples include the four I feel are easiest to create for online business newbies. They're the types of businesses I've started, as have my friends, family, and the folks I interviewed for my Lifestyle Business Mastermind website. They also follow the 4S Model of lifestyle business design because they are easy to *setup*, *small* in operation, easy to *scale* and, once they're up and running, they become *secondary* to your lifestyle goals.

They are set it and forget it businesses—set them up, find your niche and express mastery at whatever it is you're doing. Outsource what you can and walk away.

Collect a monthly paycheck.

Chapter Fifteen
Model #1—Drop Shipping

"You were born to win, but to be a winner, you must plan to win, prepare to win, and expect to win."

~ Zig Ziglar

One of the more popular online business models is *drop shipping*. The drop-shipping model is one where you, the retailer, have an online store but no inventory. You may have a laptop in a hostel, a desktop in your bedroom, or an iPad in your dorm room—it doesn't matter. As long as you can set up a storefront, you can be a successful eTailer.

How? Because you create a drop-ship company where another supplier (maybe in Singapore, Seattle, or anywhere) *drops* (pulls the item from their shelves) and *ships* (sends it out on your behalf) for you. This business models allows you to sell a variety of products from a variety of storefronts or one central storefront, without having to invest in a warehouse or inventory.

Here's my simple and basic lifestyle business design definition:

DROP SHIPPING—*an online store with no inventory. Transfers the customer order and shipment details to a manufacturer or wholesaler who then ships the goods directly to the customer.*

The key component? You are operating an online store without inventory. You take the orders, hand them off, and the manufacturer or wholesaler does the rest.

This model provides a majority of the benefits of operating a retail (etail) business without the hassles and significant investment of stocking inventory.

Not to mention the headaches.

The drop-ship method relies on four critical components:

THE CUSTOMER—A potential customer finds your online store and places an order:

YOU—you, the storeowner, or etailer transfers the order to:

THE DROP SHIPPER—the person fulfilling the order, pulling it from the shelves, packaging, and shipping it to the customer.

THE PAYMENT PROCESSOR—the merchant or banker who receives payment from the customer. Customers place orders, but, before it can be fulfilled, they must provide payment information. When the payment processor 'processes', verifies the information, and approves the purchase, the order containing shipping information is transferred to the drop-shipping company.

When the payment is processed, it is divided three ways:

- The payment processor takes a small percentage per transaction.
- The drop-shipping company takes a larger percentage for their considerable efforts, which is paid by the payment processor.
- You receive the rest.

Do you see? You don't do most of the work when choosing this business model. In fact, the customer does more work than you in this model!

The bulk of the work is performed by the drop-shipping company and, to a lesser degree, the payment processors.

Now, let's look at a few pros and cons of this model as it applies to your lifestyle—as you consider them, think about how the pros will work for you, and how the cons may work against you.

PROS OF THE DROP SHIP
BUSINESS MODEL

NO INVENTORY OR STOCK. Inventory is a huge investment—ask any brick-and-mortar person. Drop shipping means the stock comes from somewhere else, so you don't have to worry about it.

NO ORDER FULFILLMENT. Processing orders, pulling stock, and running from one end of the warehouse to the other takes time. Which is why I attempt to dissuade individuals from operations such as eBay.

Do you want to spend a good portion of your day running around to the post office and back? I doubt it! Gas prices are high, and time to run errands is at a premium—drop shipping makes good use of your time, and it can be a viable lifestyle business.

CONS OF THE DROP SHIP
BUSINESS MODEL

HIGHER INITIAL COSTS. Compared to the other business models we'll be covering, drop shipping will have a slightly higher cost to enter the business. For instance—there are typically more up-front costs associated with an ecommerce site, as opposed to a simple website.

You may want to rent a platform such as Shopify.com in order to get off the ground quickly. Using such software as a service platform ties you to a high monthly fixed cost. That might be okay if you're earning money—but it may be too high if your sales are still low.

A 'real payment gateway' requires set-up fees instead of using something like PayPal. While you can opt to use PayPal, most ecommerce sites typically use a real gateway such as Authorize.net and a merchant account.

B2C SUPPORT. I like to work business to business because they are lower maintenance than consumers. When you're selling to consumers (B2C), they require a little more TLC when it comes to customer support—which translates to *time consuming*. If time is the priority based on your Rockstar Trifecta, you may want to consider a different type of online business. Remember—it doesn't do you any good to settle for something that may not be right for you.

9 KEY FACTORS TO CONSIDER BEFORE COMMITTING TO A DROP-SHIP MODEL

The drop-ship model isn't for everyone. While potentially lucrative and easy to automate, it's not a guaranteed shoe-in for finding customers for your product. So, before committing to a drop-ship model, there are nine key factors to consider:

1. **CUSTOMER SEGMENTS**—*customers in your particular niche who want to buy goods online.* Who are your customers? What product are they seeking? Ask yourself who wants to buy your product online versus the traditional manner of shopping. Remember, online shopping or a particular niche product isn't for everyone. Seniors may not shop online as much as younger customers, so you may not want to sell senior products online.

2. **VALUE PROPOSITIONS.** *Shop in the privacy of your home, and find products related to a narrow niche.* People who find you will want what you're selling, and they'll want to buy it online. These two factors should narrow what you're selling, as well as your potential customer. To avoid competing on price, I recommend products that aren't widely sold.

Find a narrow niche that only you or very few people serve.

3. **SALES CHANNELS.** *Online only, but you could expand to taking orders over the phone.* The goal for an online businesses is to work less and sell more and, in some cases, the goal is to identify new sales channels you can expand offline, as well. For instance, let's say you sell hearing aids to individuals over fifty—you might do a fraction of your business online, but with an 800 number on your hearing aid website you might double or triple your online sales. A growing number of people feel more comfortable talking to a real person—especially seniors. To make it easier on yourself, consider outsourcing the phone orders to a call center that takes the calls and handles those for you.

4. **GOOD CUSTOMER RELATIONS.** *Focus on retention and product suite.* It may seem as if you can easily build a website and potential customers will visit it. You're right—they will. Focusing on customer retention (getting the same customers to come back to order from you again) is critical in the drop ship business model, and careful planning will help you achieve this critical goal before you start. If you have an online store, consider a newsletter that goes out weekly or monthly to customers who purchase from you. The newsletter can feature articles, informational tidbits, or whatever may

appeal to their interests. The best part is you can outsource the newsletter through a company that personalizes newsletters for others.

5. **REVENUE STREAMS.** *Stock up on frequently sold items to achieve a higher margin.* With drop shipping, you are sharing the profits on each sale with the drop shipping company *and* the payroll-processing merchant. That means you will make less on each sale than if you had invested in stock, warehouse, and storage. And if you were shipping it yourself. *Expect lower margins over time!* The good news is you can increase margins by focusing on your most sold items. For instance, let's say you serve a niche market and one of your products consistently outsells other products by a margin of five to one. If increasing profit is your goal, you should stock up on this item, store them in your home, and fulfill the orders yourself to avoid sharing so much of the profit. Again, this goes against the mobility and time corners of the Rockstar Trifecta—however, mobility and time are fluid so it is an option.

6. **KEY AND IMPORTANT RELATIONSHIPS.** *Stable hosting/platform with optional outsourced sales team.* When you operate an online store, a key resource is a stable hosting platform for your website so it's always live, always available to take orders, and always working smoothly. This is your bread

and butter, so don't scrimp by hiring an unreliable company! You can also take advantage of an outsourced sales team to increase revenue when you need it the most.

7. **KEY ACTIVITIES.** *Managing products, marketing, and order fulfillment*: Although you don't typically have items in stock, be aware of items that are moving. Why clutter up your online store with products no one wants? Instead, focus on what's working—i.e., manage your products. Insist on fluid communication between your payment processing and drop-ship providers so you're not shipping items that aren't paid for—or, not shipping items that are paid for! Think about customer support—while it can be outsourced, in the beginning you may want to manage customer support in an effort to understand common customer complaints. When you listen and understand a customer's complaint, you can address them in an FAQ page on your website.

8. **KEY PARTNERSHIPS.** *Drop shipper, and networks such as Facebook and Google AdWords.* Your primary partnership focus should be on establishing a relationship with a reputable drop-shipping company. Source various advertising partners, as well. Check out Google AdWords or Facebook's promotion program—you pay for services, so weighing ROI is critical. By determining

how much it costs to attract one new customer, you can pinpoint if you're still making a profit. You'll know if the ad site is worth it, or if you need to find something different. For instance, via one advertising channel you find you're spending thirty dollars per first-time customer—but, your sales metrics show the average first-time customer spends forty-five dollars. You're profiting fifteen bucks from that advertising program! Through scaling and with more advertising, you can increase that fifteen-dollar profit via additional multiples.

9. **COST STRUCTURE.** *Variable cost (per product and marketing). Low, fixed costs (hosting and payment processor).* Drop-shipping success occurs on a sliding scale when you have low fixed costs such as your web hosting and payment processor. However, variable costs on each product sold can increase or decrease the amount of ad space.

I encourage you to consider the pros and cons each time you consider a lifestyle business—even if you already have a successful online business. Remember, situations change and your life may not be the same as when you began your first business.

PARTING THOUGHTS . . .
A PROBING QUESTION

Drop shipping isn't a complicated business model, but it does require your considering various factors before determining if it's right for you. Ask yourself this question—*do I have any ideas for physical products that I can sell this way?*

How you answer this question will help determine if drop shipping is the right business model for you.

Chapter Sixteen
Model #2—Online Services

*"In order to succeed, your desire for success
should be greater than your fear of failure."*
~ Bill Cosby

Online services: *web agency selling online
services or solutions such as website creation,
search engine optimization, or design services.*

Many people feel they need to be a computer
geek, online guru, or software programmer to make
this business model work. Not so—outsource to the
geeks, gurus, and programmers! That's the beauty of
it! Remember—if you can't do it, there's always
someone out there who can.

The service oriented business model can be
quite lucrative—I know. I have several in this

category. I have a search engine optimization (SEO) company for the Danish market, and I outsource all of the production. Yes, I still do a little client support, but only a few hours a month—max!

This business model requires you to offer a specific service such as designing a website, setting up a blog, or creating romance book covers. First, provide the service. Second, hand it over. For instance:

WEB DESIGN

If you design a website or setup a blog for a customer, it's wise to build a monthly maintenance fee into the contract. Once a week, you may spend an hour or less updating information and, if you desire, the maintenance can be automated. In return, you're earning passive income on every past, present and future website or blog you design. That's a pretty good deal! If you're hanging in there with your nine to five, is it possible for you to earn passive money on your efforts on a particular project? No! The sad part is it never will be possible—ever. When you have blockade such as a nine to five standing in your way, do you have what it takes to take a different path? Of course you do!

COVER DESIGN

If you are offering a book cover design service, create a website with a few sample covers. Then, as orders come in, delegate the projects to a trusted core of graphic designers (check out various outsourcing sites such as oDesk.com.)

For you, the beauty of such service business models is there is periodic and piecemeal work involved. Initial time outlay will be a day or two for setting up the site, and an hour or two a day or week maintaining it. Depending on the quality of time you put in, you can easily be operating a thriving service business in no time!

Remember Yamile? She weighed mobility high in the Rockstar Trifecta, and she was doing all of the work herself. I'm weighing time higher than mobility—therefore, my companies typically use outsourcing for the production aspect in order to help me free up more time. Yamile's and my priorities are examples of different views of the same model—make certain you explore which corner of the Rockstar Trifecta motivates you!

But, as you know, there are always pros and cons, and if you don't write down every one you can think of, you're not doing yourself a service. In fact, you'll be doing yourself a disservice. Once you gain momentum as you're writing down the pros and cons, you'll see just how many pros there are!

PROS OF THE ONLINE SERVICES
BUSINESS MODEL

POTENTIAL HIGH MARGIN

When you outsource or automate the bulk of the online services you provide, there's potential for a high profit margin. Based on the designer's fees, you will know what cost to pass on to your customer—100% or more depending on your services and clientele.

NO PRODUCTS, NO RETURNS

Since you're creating a personalized service for each client, there aren't any products to ship—that means no returns! Can you imagine the effort of taking orders, shipping them, and then having your customer return the item? It's not a pretty sight, and it will suck up more time that you probably have to give. You also have to think about the time of your customer, not only your time. Do you like taking the time to return something you purchased in good faith? It's a drag—so it can't possibly be a win-win situation if you *and* your customer hate returns!

When you think about an online service that will fit your rockstar lifestyle, factor in the ease with which you can operate your business. If you find yourself wasting time with errands or aspects of the business that aren't time effective, figure out if that business is for you.

CONS OF THE ONLINE SERVICES
BUSINESS MODEL

DIFFICULT TO SCALE

You will be actively involved during the initial process of selling to each client and providing first-in-line support. Not automating means meeting or talking with clients, and servicing their needs can be time consuming. Remember, the better the delivery process setup, the more you can build your business to be scalable.

QUALITY DEPENDS ON THE PROVIDER

Once you reel in clients, sell them on your service, and make them feel comfortable with your process such as the project transitions to an actual provider. Finding the right team to provide quality service is critical to avoid complaints of poor quality later on. The team concept is prevalent throughout businesses, large or small, and it's important to make the most of synergistic energy that is a natural result of great teamwork.

Make the most of it!

9 KEY FACTORS TO CONSIDER BEFORE
COMMITTING TO AN ONLINE SERVICES MODEL

Before committing to an online services model, there are nine key factors to consider:

1. **QUALITY CUSTOMER SEGMENTS.** *Target small businesses.* If you target individuals, you may run into pay walls or problems with nonpayment. However, if you target small businesses, they usually have the money to pay for your services. Find a niche that isn't served and serve it. For instance, you may be able to specialize in creating websites specifically for carpenters, or doing ecommerce sites for local retailers.

2. **VALUE PROPOSITIONS.** *You can compete on price because you're outsourcing.* Remember, since you're not doing the work yourself, you can hire affordable contractors (designers, editors, programmers, etc.) to do the work for you. That means you can compete on price. You can also focus on a skill set beyond the client's reach. What does that mean? Well, a carpenter can build a great set of cabinets, but designing his own website to attract more customers is usually beyond his reach.

Finally, create value—not headaches—by offering specific services for a specific, fixed rate. For custom projects when you're working hourly for due dates and deliverables, it becomes time consuming and hard to automate. However, if you offer a web design package that comes in silver, bronze, and platinum levels, the client knows what they're getting and contractors know what they're providing.

Everyone's happy!

3. **SALES CHANNELS.** *Local businesses.* This is simple—target local businesses. You can physically target them, or you can build online traffic through search engine optimization by implementing target keywords for your specific niche.

4. **CUSTOMER RELATIONS.** *Automated. Self-service.* The goal with this business model is to target a specific niche, secure customers, and outsource the work. Consider automated and self-service options, and only get personally involved on high-level, custom sales. For instance, you can create help files, documents, or PDF files. FAQs, audio files, or video files help walk clients through various steps of signing up for your service. This requires some upfront effort on your part, but, once recorded, filmed, or written you can set it and forget it for optimum automation. If your personal contact is needed, it can be processed through email, text, or phone. Skype works well, too. For the sake of mobility and time, limit your contact options to email and text—doing so will allow you to service clients while traveling or on vacation.

5. **REVENUE STREAMS.** *Favor services with recurring payments.* Regardless of the business model you're using, it's easier to try to sell to existing clients rather than finding a new client to

sell to for the first time, so try to favor services with recurring payments. Try to upsell when possible.

For example, provide 'x' amount of articles featuring SEO per month, or offer to update websites with blog posts (or other features) each month after your initial design. Instead of a one-off sale, you have a recurring sale with subsequent recurring payments. Think of yourself as a broker between your service provider (the person who does the work) and the customer (the person paying for the services).

6. **KEY RESOURCES.** *The service provider. The delivery process.* Your service provider is a key resource in this business model, as well as a key partner. It's critical to map out the delivery process from start to finish because success doesn't occur until the service is delivered. If you can define and map out a quality, repeatable, and reliable delivery process, you'll be well on your way to succeeding with this business model.

7. **KEY ACTIVITIES.** *Defining the process or product, quality control, and optional consultancy.* Because you are delivering a service at a fixed price, you must define the process or product— customers need to know what they're getting, and what they're not getting. By doing this, you'll determine your profit on each transaction. For example, if you're offering an entire ecommerce

solution for a small business website, the customer can expect x, y, and z from you. You can also expect the customers do some of the work themselves, such as writing the product offerings or providing pictures of each product to be sold.

Quality control is equally important—if you're outsourcing the work, its quality must be spot-checked to avoid complaints or dissatisfied customers.

Bottom line—choose your providers wisely!

8. **KEY PARTNERSHIPS.** *Service providers.* When offering online services, you act as a broker between two parties—the service provider and the customer. Your key partners are the service providers, so treat them well. It has to be a win-win situation—they have to make money, and you have to make money. If they're not making money (or, enough money), chances are they won't be your provider for long. When things go wrong be sure to share the blame with the provider, or keep them out of it altogether. If you blame the provider every time something goes wrong, they'll stop providing.

Bummer.

9. **COST STRUCTURES.** *Variable cost.* To succeed in this business model, you should pay your service provider per project. This way you'll have a firm cost structure in place, and you'll know exactly what you're going to make on each product. And,

what it will cost you. Without a handle on how much you have to fork out for a provider, you have little chance of being as successful as you can be.

PARTING THOUGHTS . . .
A PROBING QUESTION

Ask yourself—*do I have any ideas for services or solutions I think can be sold this way?*

How you answer this question will help determine if offering online services is the right business model for you.

Make certain you address all of your concerns and doubts before making your decision.

Chapter Seventeen
Model #3—Affiliate Marketing

"You can't ask customers what they want and then try to give that to them. By the time you get it built, they'll want something new."
~ Steve Jobs

Affiliate marketing—*your promoting someone else's product or service, and making a commission for each sale you help bring to the table.*

What does that mean? Just this—you are marketing on behalf of another product or partner, and you're earning a commission for each customer you drive to your partner's site. Many believe affiliate marketing is based on leads only. However, you don't make money on leads—you make money on them only if they convert to actual customers. Some affiliate marketing partners offer money per lead such as the finance and insurance industries, but most of the time, this is not—not—the rule.

Here's an example of affiliate marketing: you offer a 'buy through' link to Amazon.com on your book review website (we'll talk more about Amazon.com later in this chapter.) Every time someone clicks on the link and buys a book from Amazon.com through that link, you get a small percentage. A commission. A commission for that purchase and everything else they stuff in their cart! If you send them to a book and they end up buying a washing machine, you get quite a nice commission!

Let's say you set up an affiliate-marketing site for a protein powder, WeightShake. Your website should focus on fitness, bodybuilding, and, perhaps, muscle enhancement with a variety of product links. Blog posts about the positive effects of protein powder of your product "WeightShake" are a good idea. Of course, not every graphic on the page will be about WeightShake, but every link will lead a potential customer somewhere where the site is making money. And, in addition to being an affiliate site for WeightShake, the blog might feature GoogleAds, which also pays a commission on every click-through purchase. In addition, they'll provide a free newsletter—a more concentrated version of the blog with articles and more WeightShake ads.

This may not be a blog or website the same people visit every day, but there is just enough information, facts, and keyword-rich material to draw hundreds—thousands—of people in every day. If a percentage of those thousands click through the various WeightShake ads daily, imagine the revenue produced by this affiliate marketplace site!

Affiliate marketing is easy entry since it has a low barrier in terms of resources, time, money, and skills. In fact, the barrier for entry is so low and the ease of use so easy, I'm seeing a lot of young people in their teens doing successful affiliate marketing, so if a teenager can do it, you can do it, too! I enjoy teaching students of all ages about lifestyle businesses, and I know how entrenched we are in our routines (such as a 9-5) as we get older. We become more inflexible and more unwilling to change. I get it— I understand it. But, I refuse to succumb to it! Do you?

PROS OF THE AFFILIATE MARKETING BUSINESS MODEL

EASY TO SET UP

When compared to the other three business models we're discussing in this section, affiliate marketing is the easiest to set up. It consists of your having a website, and signing that website address up with an affiliate-marketing program.

LOW START-UP COST

Website. Affiliate marketing program. That's it. That's your buy-in to this business—you don't need an expensive ecommerce solution, pay service providers, or an outsource company.

CONS OF THE AFFILIATE MARKETING
BUSINESS MODEL

NO CUSTOMER LOCK IN

It's hard to build loyalty or repeat service in this business model because it's designed for traffic flow—not a traffic circle. Once you send traffic to your affiliate-marketing product, service, or program, your part of the flow is over. The interaction then becomes between whom you referred and the relative product. That's why you earn a commission—for driving traffic, and not interacting with it.

LOW LEVEL OF CONTROL

As an outside observer or traffic controller for someone else's product, you have a very low-to-no level of control over that product. For instance, if the makers of the product decide to yank it off the market, change the price, or start producing it with less quality, then you're out of that loop and you have no say in the matter. They may also decide, at any time, to change the terms of the affiliate-marketing agreement so you make less commission per transaction. Again, there's very little you can do about it— you stay or leave the program.

9 KEY FACTORS FOR CONSIDERING THE AFFILIATE-MARKETING MODEL

Affiliate marketing is all about scale—the more traffic you generate to your affiliate partner, the more profit you make for your efforts. However, before committing to an affiliate-marketing model, there are nine key factors to consider:

1. **CUSTOMER SEGMENTS.** *Very narrow niche market.* Since you will be relying on search engine optimization as your primary traffic driving strategy, the more refined you can make your niche, the better it will suit your entry into this business model. So, look for a very narrow niche to fill.

For example—to help narrow your niche, consider checking out Amazon.com and looking at various specialty magazines, catalogs, or books. If there is a particular specialty with one or more magazines devoted to it, you can bet money is being spent in that niche, and people are shopping online for that product.

2. **VALUE PROPOSITIONS.** *Provide additional value to the product for which you are an affiliate.*

Remember—your website must complement the actual website of your affiliate partner (who will be talking about and serving the same narrow niche).

Ask yourself this question—*why will anyone visit my site first before clicking through to the main site?* It's a good question. In order to funnel potential customers to your site, concentrate on providing additional content that isn't available on your affiliate's site. Perhaps a product review, or an online tutorial for how to use the product.

Think about this—you are an affiliate for a given software product, and you earn 30% on each sale of that software product. You then create a blog where you upload videos that educate potential customers about how to use the product. An *affiliate link* is each link to the product on your page that goes to the external product order. By providing an affiliate link, you are providing value to the reader of your blog. It's a win-win situation. A well-known successful affiliate marketer is doing a lot of this—in his most recent income report, he made almost $3,000 in a single month on a single software product. The link next to the main product link was his—a webinar where people learned how to use the product to find profitable niches.

3. **SALES CHANNELS.** *Website with good SEO. Optional paid traffic.* Search engine optimization, or SEO, will be the main sales channel for this business

model. Having a website crammed with SEO keywords committed to your affiliate product will help your site be an initial stop on the path to finding the product itself. You can also dabble with paying for traffic, but remember your profit is dependent on each customer you send to the affiliate site. The downside is the more you pay for that to happen, the less profit goes in your pocket.

4. **CUSTOMER RELATIONS.** *Website only.* In affiliate marketing, your website is a rest stop on a customer's journey to the affiliate website. There is little-to-no customer contact. You may have a contact form on your website but, for the most part, it's just for show.

5. **REVENUE STREAMS.** *Information products can return up to 70% commission.* If you are driving traffic to an information product, such as a self-help series, ebook series, or a tutorial series, you can realize up to a 70% commission on each sale. That's a lot of ROI in any business, let alone these four business models we've been discussing! For a great example of the types of information products associated with affiliated marketing go to www.ClickBank.com—you'll see a wide array of what I'm talking about. If you are an affiliate for the popular and credible etailer, Amazon.com, you earn less commission—in the range of 4% to10 %—but since Amazon.com is so well-trusted and it makes it

so easy for customers to buy, the chances of making more sales per day increase exponentially.

6. **KEY RESOURCES.** *Website, and any content you produce for added value.* Affiliate marketing begins and ends with your website, but you may decide to offer a variety of added value with your site such as blogs, reviews, or commentaries.

7. **KEY ACTIVITIES.** *Managing the affiliate products. SEO. Creating added value.* Occasionally, the affiliate product may change its price, cover design, or other features. It's important to update any product information on your website, as well as develop SEO content to drive traffic. And, you have the option of offering added value, such as a special report, online tutorial . . .

8. **KEY PARTNERSHIPS.** *The affiliate program. Optional outsourced team for creating SEO or added value content.* Your key partnership in this business model will be your affiliate program—remember to check out ClickBank.com, CJ.com, and others. You may want to outsource for SEO or added value content.

9. **COST STRUCTURE.** *Low initial cost.* Affiliate marketing is a perfect avenue for those starting out with an online business model to try and get their feet wet. Low entry barrier!

PARTING THOUGHTS . . .
A PROBING QUESTION

Ask yourself—*do I know any cool products for which I can build a site—and, make money on sales?* If so, affiliate marketing may be the right business model for you!

Chapter Eighteen
Model #4—Information Products

"Business opportunities are like buses, there's always another one coming."

~ Richard Branson

Now, let's look at the fourth business model—information products. When you choose this lifestyle model, you'll be selling your knowledge. Think about your passion—what you know—and how you can sell your knowledge about it to others.

Information products:

> *Packaging your knowledge, and selling it to people in order to provide them with information on a specific topic.*

Many people learn about and realize the ultimate rockstar lifestyle business by selling informational products online. Information, unlike drop shipping or selling a service such as graphic design or web design, you simply 'post' it (format your ebook, webinar, or informational video), 'host' it (give it a virtual address, website, or blog host), and 'toast' it (celebrate the passive income that results)!

Of course, there is a little more to it than that, but the fact remains that dealing in information takes your expertise—whatever that may be—and monetizes it once you've created an information product like a webinar, video series, or ebook to sell.

When considering the business model of selling informational products, think about these three excellent examples:

- A nail salon tech who monetizes her expertise by posting five-minute tutorials on special nail designs—prom night, Halloween, or New Year's Eve. First date, wedding, or Christmas. She charges $4.99 a pop, or she has a channel where you subscribe for $.99 a month, and you'll have access to five videos during that month. It's a significant savings for you, but imagine the kind of Rockstar Lifestyle business she's running if only a few thousand people subscribe at less than a dollar per month.

- The romance author who writes a new novella a month, selling them for $1.99, and creating a legion of fans with the occasional contest or freebie.

- The expert author who writes about topics in a particular niche such as management, IT, or recruiting. Perhaps the author writes about human resources, nursing, or landscaping. Finding and promoting to the right niche audience ensures you always have a loyal audience for your work.

You might think you need to be high on the education ladder for this business model, but not so. We all know a little bit about many things, and every one of us knows of one particular niche we can fill—photography, weight loss, or movies. Finances, real estate, or cars. Your niche is special to your passion, and it will be your first step to determine whether jumping into the information products game is for you.

PROS OF THE INFORMATION PRODUCTS BUSINESS MODEL

GOOD PROFIT MARGINS

Unlike physical information products such as printed books, DVDs and CDs, digital products have no costs associated with them after you create them, and that leaves the door open for healthy profit margins.

EASY DELIVERY

With just a few clicks, your digital information product can be in the hands of your customers in seconds, not minutes.

LOW STARTUP COSTS

The basic requirement for entering the information products game is a website, a payment button, and a delivery system to get the product to your customer. That's it. If you're looking for a lifestyle business that's cheap, then this may be the perfect solution for you. It's always important to keep your budget in mind—you're starting a new venture, and it's silly to spend a boatload of money on it before you know if it's something that sparks your passion and if it will be successful.

CONS OF THE INFORMATION PRODUCTS BUSINESS MODEL

TIME CONSUMING

It usually takes some time to write a quality book, or to record a quality DVD or audio series for which people will shell out some bucks.

REQUIRES SUBJECT KNOWLEDGE

You have to know the topic before you can help other people benefit from it. Your customers will determine quickly if you're knowledgeable and an expert in your topic. If you come across as unconfident and struggling regarding the topic, you can bet the customer won't refer you. Ever.

9 KEY FACTORS TO CONSIDER BEFORE COMMITTING TO AN INFORMATION PRODUCTS MODEL

Before committing to the information products model, there are nine key factors to consider:

1. CUSTOMER SEGMENTS. *Narrow niche.* Customers turn to ebooks, podcasts, and video tutorials for assistance, and there are many people providing information. Competition. However, you can do well for yourself if you choose a narrow niche, and serve it well.

2. VALUE PROPOSITIONS. *You must provide value through high quality content.* There is a vast difference in the quality of information products on the market today. I see a growing trend of people buying already written material and passing it off as their own. They use royalty-free or free content, packaging it as a product, and sell it themselves. However, to make this business model an income-

generating proposition rather than a cash grab, it's critical to provide quality and originally produced content. Become an expert, and position yourself with quality content that provides real value—a value they can recommend to friends and family. There is also value by synthesizing complex information for the consumer market. For instance, there may be hundreds of research papers on the health pitfalls of drinking soda, but who has the time to go through them? If you can go through them, however, and synthesize and summarize the complex material for consumers in a simple fifty-page report, there's value in positioning the findings in an accessible format.

3. **SALES CHANNELS.** *Ebooks, membership sites, newsletters, and webinars.* There are various sales channels involved in the information products business models—ebooks (you may not be able to charge as much as a printed book, but you can sell more at a reasonable price.) Membership sites (you have recurring monthly or regular fees, and you offer interactivity via podcasts, FAQs, and videos.) Free newsletters can drive customers toward your main informational products—they view it as added value, as well as proof of your expertise and credibility. Finally, you can use webinars as lead generators to your main informational product, or you can film a video interview with individuals asking questions about your topic. When you compile enough footage

(about an hour), you can package the video and sell it.

4. **CUSTOMER RELATIONS.** *Usually automated, potential for interaction and growth.* With the information product business model, you will create an information product and sell it online, so the customer relationship barrier is low. However, there are multiple opportunities to add value and generate leads by creating interactive videos or other multimedia. Maybe you are a coach, and clients pay for your time—which is, of course, highly interactive and consumer focused. Finally, you can partner with other experts in your field—tap into their audiences to grow your own. For instance, invite a fellow expert to participate in your webinar, feature it on the expert's site for exposure, and grow your audience through the joint partnership.

5. **REVENUE STREAMS.** *Asset sale vs. recurring sale.* For the majority of information products such as ebooks or a DVD series, the customer buys and you get paid. Membership sites or affiliate partnerships offer opportunities for recurring sales, so build an information product to create recurring revenue—a product suite. For example, offer a webinar series and a tutorial video in conjunction with the ebook.

6. **KEY RESOURCES.** *Your knowledge, your website, an editor for your website.* How you present your knowledge will drive potential customers to your website. If you aren't the best at writing, or you need someone to check your writing for errors—grammar, spelling, punctuation, and sentence structure—it's wise to hire a freelancer who's an expert. It doesn't have to cost much if you turn to a site such as Elance.com—you'll post your project and receive bids from contractors. You have the option to post your budget, so you can be certain to keep your costs at a minimum. Remember, a website that's filled with errors turns off the majority of site visitors.

7. **KEY ACTIVITIES.** *Creating content.* Content is key in the information products business model. Customers pay you for it—quality content unique and special to you and your niche. Take time to write and produce quality content! You will also want to market your information product so more people buy it more often—update your website to offer product reviews, excerpts, or graphics. Think about offering something interactive such as audio and video. Remember—you want customers to refer to your information product as a quality product.

8. **KEY PARTNERSHIPS.** *Optimally benefit from joint venture partnerships in order to reach bigger audiences.* Placing an ebook, audio, or video product

for sale on the internet doesn't equate to sales—you must drive traffic to the product so people know about it and, sometimes, it takes joint venture partnerships. You can share a portion of the proceeds with peers, colleagues, or fellow authors who drive traffic to your site. This way, people find out about your product and you pay a small percentage to the person who referred the customer. In effect, you become the affiliate partner, and they drive the traffic to you!

9. COST STRUCTURE. *Low initial cost or entry barrier.* Other than the time it takes to produce quality content, there is little-to-no cost to enter the information product business beyond the fixed costs of maintaining a website.

PARTING THOUGHTS . . .
A PROBING QUESTION

Finally, ask yourself this question:

Do I have any knowledge for which people are willing to pay? If so, you may have found your calling! Remember—people will pay to find out what others know.

Information rules.

PART 5

The Next Step

Chapter Nineteen
Finding Your Passion

"Do what you did, and you get what you got."

~Unknown

Well, you made it to the final words of this book. So—where should you start? We've been through several business models, but a business isn't only a model—you still need to put your own business ideas into it. But, how do you figure out what market to approach, and what kind of customers you should target?

Some people might label this chapter "Finding Your Niche", which is perfectly valid. The only trouble I have with the word *niche* is it sounds like it's something secret or sacred—and, when discovered, it will turn into the proverbial pot of gold at the end of the rainbow.

I believe niche is used too much—*if you discover the right niche then your fortune will be made.* People who write about finding a niche typically do so from a scientific standpoint—they're seeking a formula for how successful a potential niche will be. That said, I'll present you with scientific ways of validating your market, but I don't feel these should ever stand alone. Nope—instead, I've labeled this chapter *Finding Your Passion*—it's what you need to do.

PASSION KICKS ASS

When it comes to building your lifestyle business, you should find a subject about which you are passionate. Let's face it—you can make money on most things. If you're passionate about it, chances are there are other people out there who share your passion—and they'll be willing to put money on it.

There is a difference between *interested in* and *passionate about*—people might be interested in toilet paper, but few are passionate about it.

Another reason it's good to find something you're passionate about is it will keep you motivated. Many times, you need to experience trial and error to get to the point of making money in your lifestyle business. If you're not really passionate about it, your chances of quitting are higher.

Building a lifestyle business is a long-term lifestyle choice—not a get-rich-quick business. Because it's a lifestyle choice, turning your hobby into a business is a better strategy than following a checklist and ending up pushing clogs for Canadian woodworkers just because you discovered a hole in the market and the 'perfect niche'. Think about it— we're knowledgeable about things that interest us.

We're knowledgeable about our passions.

This means you will have a head start—let's say you're building a drop-ship business within a market about which you are passionate. You probably already know which products are best and you have an idea of the competition. The fact is you already know more than others. If you know nothing about the market and products, you have to learn it—all of it. While it's easy to suck in information, it becomes boring if you have no interest in the market or product.

Imagine you're a tax accountant. You can launch a service (product) helping individuals with their personal taxes at a fixed yearly price. Once setup, develop a checklist so someone else other than you performs the actual work.

Here's another example of a business that may work for you—create an informational product such as an ebook on how to optimize your personal finances. Heck, you could give the ebook away for free if people signed up for your email newsletter— then advertise your service to the people on the list and, in the end, sell a higher-priced product than the simple ebook.

Hopefully, I have sold you the idea that you should be passionate about the subject of your business. Does this mean you can sell any product in any market? No, of course not—there should be a viable market that is willing to pay money for whatever you're planning to offer. For this, however, we need to turn to a more scientific approach . . . more on this later.

What is your passion? What do you love to do and spend countless hours doing it? Can you imagine your passion as a lifestyle business?

SLIM THAT BABY DOWN!

There's big money in fitness and in personal finance. Does that mean that you should develop a product in one of these markets? Maybe—are you passionate about it?

The answer is yes and no (sorry—more confusing is probably not what you need right now!)

These are big markets with thousands of players, so how do you stand a chance of getting your own message out there? How can you persuade people to buy your product, and not those of your competitors'? This is why people talk about niche sites—'niching down'. It means going after one small segment of a bigger market.

Success story—Steve Kamb, developer of NerdFitness.com. He took a saturated niche with thousands of competitors—but, he directed his voice and marketing toward desk jockeys, nerds, and Average Joes (his words).

The blog, NerdFitness.com, hit the internet in 2009 and, while there aren't official numbers, Steve is doing well for himself these days—he's reached the status of operating one of the most trafficked websites in the U.S. This success is by one who says he isn't a fitness expert! Oh, yes—he admits it. Steve penetrated an overcrowded market, and angled it toward a specific segment within that market. You got it—niching down.

So how much should you slim your business? As much as possible. Consider: the more you narrow your target business . . .

—the better match it will be for someone who stumbles upon your site

—it will increase the number of potential customers

The idea is to make your niche as narrow as possible while maintaining your marketplace. It makes sense—if you enter into a market that houses thousands of others in your niche, you may compromise your chances of achieving your goals.

RUNNING DOWN THE NUMBERS

Now—the scientific approach. Remember, I recommend choosing a business about which you are passionate. This section will help you validate your choice or, perhaps, help you select a specific product or service.

Some years ago, there was a buzz about blue ocean strategies following the 2005 release of *Blue Ocean Strategy*. This strategy advises organizations to create new demands in uncontested market spaces (blue ocean) instead of competing directly with other companies in their industries. It may sound like a grand idea, and I often hear pitches of ideas such as 'no one ever thought of this before'.

Forget it! Instead:

—copy what's working, and

—improve it a little.

If you have a new and innovative product, you'll have to change people's habits in order to get them to buy it. Do you know how much money you will need in your marketing budget in order to get people to change their habits? Millions! That's why the Blue Ocean Strategy might be great for big corporations that have those millions, but it's utterly useless if you're a small, lifestyle business. You can't create a market without a budget. Period. So, you need to hook into an existing market for which people are already spending their dollars.

So, how can you identify existing markets? You have several choices, and the first thing to do is to make the most of Google's keyword tool:

https://adwords.google.com/o/KeywordTool.

This tool tells you what keywords people are seeking, and it suggests alternative search phrases. For example, if you search 'personal tax accountant', Google will tell you there are approximately 1.300 searches for this term every month (and, there is a great deal of competition for this keyword.) However, it will also tell you there is an alternative 'income tax accountant' phrase for which 4.400 are searching each month, and that it's a 'low competition keyword.'

Making the best use of Google Adwords is a great way to fine-tune the wording on your website. If you optimize the text on your site to correlate to

178

Finding Your Passion

the keywords for which people are searching, you have a much higher chance of people finding you through the search engines.

Keep in mind Google Adwords indicates people are interested in the subject, but it doesn't tell you whether people are spending money on it. To figure that out, you can turn to Amazon for help. If there are books about your subject, there's a good chance consumers are spending money in your chosen market.

Also, check out magazines in your particular market—if there's one magazine, I guarantee someone is spending money. I know this because a magazine needs advertisers in order to operate, and if there are advertisers, then products are selling. Simply by reviewing magazines, you can validate your market.

Do some research—find out who the players are in your chosen market. Will you have many competitors in your niche? Or, have you hit on something that can bring in some bucks? I think it applies to any business venture—perform the ever-important due diligence. Do your homework, run the numbers, and decide if there's a viable spot for your idea within the marketplace. If there is, keep moving forward. If there isn't, move on . . .

IT'S ALL ABOUT MODELS, BABY!

So, what do you do if there are many players in your chosen market? One market that comes to mind is life coaches—everybody seems to be a life coach these days. The problem is the minute they call themselves a life coach, they are competing with every other life coach out there.

So what to do then? First thing, don't call yourself a life coach—offer a solution model instead. What do I mean by solution model? Simply this—create your own model for helping people. Call it whatever you want—you can, for instance, create a model to help people with their fears. You can name it 'Fear Control System', and suddenly you aren't competing with life coaches. Instead, you have a unique product in an existing market!

Look at the giant business of Tony Robbins (which can hardly be described as a lifestyle business, although I believe he only does what he likes and he has people to do everything else). His background is in NLP (Neuro-linguistic Programming) which is all about communication, personal development, and psychotherapy. If you haven't heard of Tony Robbins, take the time to do a little research. He's an icon in the self-help arena, and he's marketed his business brilliantly—he touts himself as a 'peak performance coach' and his success is evident through his books, seminars, and television appearances.

He found his niche.

But can you see any reference of this on his website? Nope. He took what he learned and developed his own models and systems! Inspirations from NLP are evident throughout his material, but it isn't the only reason he's successful. He's a brilliant coach and businessperson.

You see, there is a distinction between developing your own products for new markets and developing new products in existing markets. If you can create a unique take and product or service within an existing market such as Steve Kamb did, then you'll find your own personal success. Your own magic.

Your own rockstar lifestyle.

Chapter Twenty
Take Action—NOW!

"Twenty years from now, you will be more disappointed by the things that you didn't do than by the ones you did do. So throw off the bowlines. Sail away from the safe harbor. Catch the trade winds in your sails. Explore. Dream. Discover."

~Mark Twain

So. Here we are. The fork in the road between opportunity and regret. You stuck with me this long, and you learned a lot in our time together—your time was not wasted.

A quick recap . . .

THE LIFESTYLE LIE. What got you here won't get you to your future—you have to understand that now is the time to act. Don't take a second or third job—create a lifestyle business.

THE ROCKSTAR TRIFECTA. The three corners of the Rockstar Trifecta include time, money, and mobility. The Rockstar Trifecta is flexible and when you control your own fate, you can spend less time on one corner of the Rockstar Trifecta, such as money, and more on time or mobility. Or, both.

THE 4S MODEL OF LIFESTYLE BUSINESS DESIGN. Any rockstar lifestyle business you design should follow the 4S Model—simple to setup, small in scope, simple to scale, and secondary to your life goals.

LIFESTYLE BUSINESS MODELING. The four most simple, basic, common, and profitable online lifestyle business models can provide enough time, money, and mobility to help you live your rockstar lifestyle. No more time clocks!

Take action now! Think about how you dream of living differently—more time, money, or mobility. Well, here's your chance!

Time passes. Don't waste time waiting for someone else to make the decision for you—what's beautiful about building a lifestyle business is the building part—you have time.

You don't have to take out a loan, sell your firstborn, or make a deal with the devil. All you have to do is take action now.

If you're unsure of which business model to adopt, relax—you can build a lifestyle design on your own schedule, at your own pace, and according to your own risk tolerance. I guarantee once you build your first storefront, find an information product that piques your interest, or a product to market, drop-ship, or sell, you will want to spend more time understanding your business, perfecting it, setting it up, and refining it.

Then, you'll reap the benefits—the benefits of money, time, and mobility. But you won't get them by doing the same things you always do. Remember—*do what you did, and you get what you got!*

It's human nature—if you don't act within a few days of inspiration, your chances of acting at all reduce with each passing day.

Why risk it?

I know change can be intimidating, particularly when you're changing things as critical as how you earn your income and your day-to-day lifestyle. But before I send you off to become the lifestyle rockstar

I know you are, let's revisit some of the people who live the rockstar lifestyle now . . .

Remember Yamile? She's the young internet entrepreneur and lifestyle business designer—in her twenties, Yamile is a true international nomad, wandering wherever she wants, and finding the time, money, and mobility to live the lifestyle of her dreams. With little overhead other than her backpack and laptop, it may seem like Yamile is a rare breed—but, as I move through my own international world, I meet more and more people like Yamile each day. Not all of them are young—they're what I call the nine-to-five dropouts—those who are much happier, less restricted, and less stressed since they stopped working for someone else and started their own lifestyle businesses. Like me, they tired of the grind and realized there was more to life than work.

Maybe they're early retirees who, instead of seeing their homes as their only investment, chose to invest in themselves by selling their homes and traveling the world while working only a few hours a week to support their new lifestyles.

Then there's Johnny Cupcakes. He found ways to be his own boss, and he succeeded in crafting his successful lifestyle business by selling t-shirts. Johnny's inspiring story proves you don't have to be a rocket scientist, or raise millions in venture capital to create a business. Most people I meet who live the same lifestyle as I are less flashy or wealthy. But, having researched Johnny Cupcakes for this book, I think he would be happy with whatever success his t-shirts found.

What's unique about Johnny Cupcakes is that he created a lifestyle business geared to what he loves—but you don't have to. As we discussed in the four lifestyle business models, since you're going to be automating or outsourcing most of the actual day-to-day work of your lifestyle business, you don't have to love what you're doing in order to earn money. You only have to love how you spend your life!

Finally, yours truly. You already know my story, but I want to bring it back into focus now because I can't emphasize enough how simple it is to start, operate, outsource, and automate a lifestyle business. I'm not extraordinarily brave, resourceful, or technical—in fact, I'm not a particularly entrepreneurial person. I'm someone who wanted something different for my life, something far from the nine-to-five pace I saw taking too much time away from my family, friends, and free time. For me, a lifestyle business wasn't about what business I wanted to start—it was about how I could create a business for passive income by using the 4S Model. It was about how quickly, affordably, and effectively I could live my lifestyle on my own terms. Now, having created multiple lifestyle businesses, I couldn't wait to share the experience with you.

Take Action—NOW!

It's up to you to make yours a rockstar lifestyle!

———————

Now is the time. Your life, dreams, family, and goals are too valuable to give up. Live the rockstar lifestyle you want by making it a priority—go after your dreams! Not tomorrow, next week, next month or next year—today! Do it now! Put down this book, pick up your mouse, and begin to build the rockstar lifestyle business of your dreams.

Now . . .

ARE YOU READY TO CHANGE YOUR LIFE?

READER ONLY!
FREE BONUS TRAINING:

The Lifestyle Business Rockstar
Training Kit

You will receive:

—3 in-depth training videos about how you can create a lifestyle business, kick ass, quit your 9-5, and live the life you truly want.

—The Lifestyle Business Passion Finder which will help you zero in on your areas of passion and competence, as well as design a plan to help you reach your dream life faster.

Visit my website to claim your free

Lifestyle Business Rockstar Training Kit:

http://LifestyleBusinessRockstar.com/BONUS

NOTES: